BUDDHA is a GREETER at Walmart

BUDDHA is a GREETER at Walmart

Using Zen in Everyday Life

KRIS NEELY

BUDDHA IS A GREETER AT WALMART
Using Zen in Everyday Life

This edition published by Zen Books Worldwide,
a Cresting Wave Publishing imprint.

ISBN: 978-0-9889048-0-4

Library of Congress Cataloging-in-Publication Data

Neely, Kris
BUDDHA IS A GREETER AT WALMART: Using Zen in Everyday Life

Summary: "The idea is simple—everyday items and situations as sources of Zen insight. From a junk drawer to a butterfly. From Ginger Rogers to Colonel Mustard. We're surrounded by items and situations which teach Zen—if we just take the time to see. Zen is a perfect antidote to the noise and untruths of daily life. Yet for many people, Zen is something that requires rigorous study, years of solitary meditation, dressing in odd garb, and quoting Buddha. Nothing could be further from the truth. Everyday life is Zen. You are the only real Zen master you'll ever need. You just need to look, see and reality will take care of the rest. Zen is everywhere and Zen is everyone—even the greeter at Walmart."—Provided by publisher.

ISBN: 978-0-9889048-0-4 (paperback)
1. Buddhism 2. Philosophy

Library of Congress Control Number: 2015905726

Cover and Interior Design by Sarah Clarehart

10 9 8 7 6 5 4 3 2 1

Dedication

This book is dedicated to my mother, Barbara Neely. Her Zen was as elegant as haiku and as manifest as a fish leaping from a still lake.

Author's Note: Impressionistic Zen

From time-to-time someone will ask me why I change or re-write famous Zen stories (koans.) First let me be very clear that I have all the respect in the world for these venerable stories/ tools and their authors. My re-writing of them or changing or adding new names or locations is not meant as disrespect, or to obscure their original text/source/author.

Think of it this way: like impressionistic painting. Not an actual life study of a painting of tulips, for example, but an impressionistic interpretation of the same.

My goal as a writer on the topic of Zen is to use my original writing/ voice as a "finger pointing at the moon" to help my readers find new insights into Buddhism and Zen. To assist in that task, I often (but not always) use "impressions" of a Zen story or koan to covey whatever point I'm writing about.

When I change names or locations or some other aspect of the original text, it's not because I'm prejudiced against Asian, Chinese, Japanese, or Indian peoples, nor am I trying to apply a Judeo or

Christian spin/slant to my writings. I'm trying to gain the reader's attention; to assist in the absorption of my impressions and message. Period—full stop.

Finally, and frankly, while I respect the rights (and copyrights) of others, I also believe that sacred cows make the best hamburger. That once some Zen/Buddhist text becomes so scared or venerable that a writer cannot use it as a basis for their impressions about their topic—it's time for a serious reconsideration. How many koans convey just such a message?

A finger pointing at the moon—that is an admirable goal for anyone raising their original voice/writing to convey impressions of Zen/Buddhism. That's my goal.

Happy reading!

Contents

Foreward:

An Introduction to This Buddha Guy

I know what some of you are thinking:

- Just who was this Buddha person, anyway?
- How did Buddha find enlightenment?
- I've been told Buddha claimed he was a god. True or false?
- What's he doing at Walmart?
- What's he selling?
- Why do I want to know what he said?
- Why should I give a hoot, anyway?

I'm glad you asked. I'm going to try to fill-in some of your blanks on the subject of Buddha and Zen. That said, my goal is not to write the definitive work on the history of Zen Buddhism per se, OK? Good.

To begin with, the man who would be known as the Buddha was, well, just a man. Born of woman, he lived, married, had a family, achieved enlightenment, spoke and taught, died, and was cremated. True, at one point in his life he was a prince, but still and all, he was—just a guy.

Buddha: The Start

Most sources indicate that the Buddha—given name Siddhartha Gautama—was born sometime between 563 and 430 BCE in what is now Nepal.

Born into royalty to his mother, Queen Maya, and his father, King Suddhodhana, young Siddhartha brought joy into a heretofore childless marriage. His father was a wealthy landowner and chief of the Shakya nation, and Siddhartha led a princely life for his first twenty-nine years*.

While Siddhartha was a baby, his father held a feast at the palace and invited a group of Brahmins (priests) so they could predict his son's future. The predictions suggested that Siddhartha would become either a great and powerful ruler or—a wise spiritual guide.

The king was not at all happy with the prediction that his son might become a spiritual leader—he wanted a son who would not only take over as king but who would expand to an even more impressive extent the empire he had built. Siddhartha's father saw him as both a warrior and heir, and in an attempt to ensure that the boy fell in line with his thinking, he made sure his son had the best of everything, every luxury imaginable. But—all strictly inside the walls of the palace.

In addition to his concerns based on the input from the Brahmins, Siddhartha's father did not want his son to venture outside and become "tainted" by contact with disease, poverty, unhappiness, or death (and what Dad would?). One story, perhaps apocryphal, has it that while Siddhartha's father ordered that the boy never even see withered or dying flowers in the palace gardens so as not to become curious about

*His father even built three palaces for his son, one for each of the three seasons in the area where they lived. Not a bad start for "just a guy."

age, death, and decay. What we do know is that Siddhartha grew into a talented athlete, a solid student under the tutelage of some of the country's best instructors, and a young man of manners and grace.

At sixteen, Siddhartha was married (as arranged by his father, of course) to a girl his own age—his cousin, and by repute the most beautiful girl in the region, Yasodhara. In time, she bore Siddhartha a son, Rahula. So far, so good, as far as his father's plan was concerned—his son was now a father himself and had secured for himself a male heir.

But—as Siddhartha grew, he also became more curious about life outside his gilded cage. One story has it that while Yasodhara was pregnant with their son, she actually suggested to Siddhartha that he seek entertainment beyond the walls of the palace.

Whatever the reason(s), Siddhartha did leave the palace, in disguise and accompanied by a servant, and ventured into the surrounding city. On his first sojourn, he is supposed to have seen a very old man, bent with the effects of age and perhaps disease. Having never before seen such a sight, Siddhartha asked Channa, his servant, why the man looked this way. Channa is said to have answered something along the lines of, "He is an old man, My Master. All men grow old." This was, so to speak, news to Siddhartha. He had never even seen a dead flower before, so what was he to make of old age in people?

On another trip beyond the palace walls, Siddhartha is said to have come upon a different man, this time quite ill and lying beside the road. Asking his servant to explain, Siddhartha was told, "The man is sick, My Master. All men can contract sickness and fall thus." Siddhartha was stunned by this news. He asked his servant if it was possible that *he*, Siddhartha, could become sick. As you might imagine, the affirmative response was another blow to Siddhartha's world. First, old age. Now, sickness? None of this was a part of *his* world. Yet these conditions were clearly a part of man's world outside the protective cocoon of the palace.

On his third trip beyond the pale, Siddhartha encountered an even more disturbing sight: a funeral procession and a man's dead body. His attendant's explanation that death was a natural part of life obviously could not have sat well with Siddhartha.

And on yet another trip outside the palace, Siddhartha came upon a monk in yellow robes with a shaved head and an empty beggar's bowl. Channa explained to Siddhartha that this man was worthy of respect for his devotion to a religious life and that, moreover, the man had renounced all worldly attachments and goods.

Siddhartha's new experiences with old age, illness, death, and the religious life triggered a most profound change in the young man. What he thought he knew about life had clearly been called into question. He now understood that there was pain and suffering in the world—and a great deal of it, as well. He'd come face-to-face with an apparently endless cycle of birth, life, pain, and death. With this education of "the ways things were", Siddhartha changed.

With his new education came a new direction for Siddhartha. He would depart his privileged place, abandon his luxurious lifestyle, leave his family and his wife and baby son, and don the shaved head and yellow robes of a monk, and try to find the answer to the cycle of birth-life-pain-death he had seen.

As the Brahmins had predicted (and his father had feared), Siddhartha was taking his first tentative steps on the spiritual path of life.

His life, his world—and ours—would never be the same again.

Buddha: Enlightenment

Wandering largely around the plain of the river Ganges, Siddhartha fell in with a small band of ascetics. He adopted many of their practices: yoga (like Zen, a way of liberation), meditation, hard work, fasting, sleeping outdoors, and other *tapas** practices. Nothing seemed to make a bit of difference—despite all his efforts, he still couldn't penetrate the mystery of relief from the cycle of birth and death known in Sanskrit as *samsara*, couldn't come to grips with his *real* self (in Sanskrit, *atman*), couldn't penetrate the transitory and illusory appearance of the physical world that obscures its actual spiritual reality (Sanskrit: *maya*), and couldn't seem to get to the base, the origin of his own mind.

Therefore, one day, after seven years of effort, he decided to relax his ascetic diet and so accepted some rice cooked in milk from a local villager. After he finished his meal, he felt some sort of change coming over him, so he resolved to sit in a meditative posture beneath a Bodhi tree and not rise until he had realized enlightenment—in other words, until he had seen ultimate reality. (A descendent of that original Bodhi tree, which regenerates itself by grounding its branches in the earth, is said to still be living in Bodh Gaya, India.)

It is said that he sat in meditation and simply *saw* the world around him—how this tree depended on the earth, how the rivers depended on the rains, how death depended on life—in short, he *saw* how the harmonious whole of existence is rooted in how every aspect *of* existence depends on every other aspect *in* existence, creating the whole, in reality.

*A Sanskrit term meaning, among other things, the austerities and practices that require sacrifice, effort, and discipline on the road to liberation, not the hors d'oeuvres served in Spanish bars and restaurants

At dawn (on the next day, or the seventh day, or just a day, depending on which account you read), Siddhartha glimpsed the morning star in the still-dark sky, and at that moment attained *anuttara samyak sambodhi*—"unexcelled, complete awakening."

He said, "Just so … I obtained not the least thing from unexcelled, complete awakening and for this very reason it is called 'unexcelled, complete awakening.'"

But in one sense, Siddhartha had, for better or for worse, obtained "something"—for the rest of his days he would be known by the honorifics he had gained as "The World Honored One," "The Buddha," "The Fully Awakened One," and "The Enlightened One."*

*To be fair, Buddhism posits that there have been Buddhas among us from the beginning. The key difference here lies in the title—not a Buddha but the Buddha, in much the same way as my title as president (of my homeowners association) is different from the president (of the United States). Although if (s)he thinks (s)he has problems as president, try dealing with a hoard of angry homeowners when the pooper scooper stations run out of bags!

Preface:

KQED Changed My Life

It's often funny, the things or events that cause someone to attempt to write a book. Sometimes it's a single word or phrase. Sometimes it's a desire to check an item off one's bucket list. In my case, it started with something a bit more prosaic: a Public Television station. I'll explain more in a moment

I'm writing this chapter on a Southwest Airlines* flight from Dallas, Texas, to Phoenix, Arizona. Sitting across the aisle from me is a wonderful woman who is by trade a physician. As a poignant example of how pervasive the use of the term "Zen" has become, the article she's reading at this moment is called "Zen and the Art of Kidney Dialysis at Home."

With apologies to kidney patients everywhere, the title of that article shows just how ingrained the use of the word "Zen" has become in today's society. Thanks largely to the book *Zen and the Art of Motorcycle Maintenance*, even the phrase "Zen and the Art of ..." has become an everyday expression.

* Southwest is my favorite airline! I even asked my ex-wife to marry me over the airplane's P.A. on a Southwest flight to Las Vegas. Now if that's not karma...

Moreover, people (even those not invested in Zen) think they know what it implies: a skillful, deep, well-thought-out spiritual approach to whatever the topic is—Zen and the Art of Underwater BB Stacking, or Zen and the Art of Flower Arranging—or even Zen and the Art of Kidney Dialysis.

Hey—it takes all kinds.

Exactly—and my approach to this book is somewhat like the use of the phrase "Zen and the Art of ..." Throughout this book I'll be using everyday situations, places, and events as well as things we see, say, do, and think at some point (or many points) in our lives, and coupling those sights, activities, or thoughts (or all of the above) with Zen teachings and Zen stories.

Part of the reason for this approach I've already explained, and the rest of the explanation is this: remember Dan Aykroyd in the movie *Trading Places?* There's a scene in which he's standing on the curb of a street, in the rain, dressed as Santa Claus, and he's down, in despair, dejected, depressed, dumped on—and a dog is taking a leak on his leg. Heck, even when he tries to shoot himself, his gun won't fire.

Well, if you're living or have lived, in some way, shape, or form, even a portion of that scene for yourself and you can't *see* Zen, in that place, time, and moment right then and right there, well, you sure as ... shootin' ... won't find Zen anywhere else, either. Zen is wherever and whenever you are—you couldn't get out of it, or get into it, if you tried. You can't find it and you can't escape from it even if you tried, either. You also can't add Zen to your life, cut back on Zen, "learn" Zen, forget Zen, or find or lose either the largest or smallest item in the known universe that isn't in Zen.

You're already in Zen, of Zen, and Zen—you just need to awaken to it, much as you have realized that you had other capabilities and attributes in life that were, at some point, unknown or unrevealed to you. At one point you didn't know how to walk, or talk, or take a shower—then something changed. Something triggered you to "see" or "understand" that you actually had such and such a skill or ability, and your response was akin to "Gee—I never knew I knew how to do that."

Zen is kind of the same way. You have it, in exactly the same measure that Buddha did 2,500 years ago—you just haven't realized or awakened to the knowledge of what you heretofore didn't know. This book will, hopefully*, be like the familiar Zen image of a finger pointing at the moon—pointing the way to your Zen, which you will clearly *see*.

And in much the same way that I would likely not comprehend the specialized language, terms, and descriptions of kidney dialysis and all things renal, I'll be translating many of the Asian and Buddhist names, places, and terms into more colloquial, everyday terms (or, editing them out when they aren't intrinsic to the topic). A student of mine once remarked that while he enjoyed Zen, he found many books on the subject a tough row to hoe because he was uncertain of the pronunciations, and as a function of that, his enthusiasm for the subject wavered. Not that you asked...

Some Zen purists may disagree with me, and that's fine, but I don't think one loses anything substantive, fails to take away anything of importance, or suffers delays in advancing their Zen training by taking this approach. I believe that the wider the circle of people I and all of us can attract to Zen, the better. But let me reiterate: I'm not teaching here, I'm pointing.

And I owe that point of view to a combination of three people: my mother, Alan Watts, and the program director of KQED-TV**,

* I can point all winter, but you have to *see*, I can't do that for you.

** KQED is the most excellent example of a classy Public Television station on the planet, IMHO.

Channel 9, San Francisco. They were the Zen travel agents on what has been a long, strange trip for me. And they brought me to you.

Mom's Home-Baked Zen

My study of Zen started with an unceremonious approach. As an (undoubtedly bright and precocious) youth, my mother plopped me down in front of our TV, tuned it to KQED Channel 9 (the PBS station serving our small, rural town of Merced, California), and said, "The program that's on next is about something called Zen. It was made by a fellow named Alan Watts. I get him. Maybe you won't, and maybe you won't understand a thing he says, but watch the program with me anyway. You might learn something."

I watched. She was right: I didn't get him. I don't know that I learned anything I can point to save this: he was *wayyyyyy* cool.

All these years later, I am still fascinated with Zen and with Alan Watts, whom I consider to be my first Zen "teacher." He was the first person to make it clear to me what Zen was and wasn't—and the first, but by no means the last, person to get me to really *see*. (You may have noticed that I sometimes italicize words, such as I just did with see. This is a device used in a number of books on Zen and Buddhism to indicate an actual, realistic activity, as opposed to an idea **about** an activity.)

But let's be clear: I'm not a Zen "guru." Or a Zen monk. Or a Zen priest. I see myself as a Zen rooster with a job to do. That's the point of this book. This work is my "cock-a-doodle-do!" Awakening? That's your job.

So let's get started.

Signed,

Kris Neely
Zen Rooster

Introduction:

Buddha Is a Greeter at Walmart

Psssst! Hey, you, reading this book: have I got some news for you. You may have already heard, but—and I've just got to get this off my chest—Buddha, you know the big "B" Buddha guy? Well, guess what?

He's a greeter at Walmart.

OK. Well, I feel better, and that's a load off my mind. Knowing the identity of an entity as profound as Buddha has been quite the burden. I mean, heck—I finally had to write a book about it.

So the next time you go to Walmart and the icon of an ancient way of liberation, The World Honored One, The Enlightened One, a man revered around the world, and the object of study and admiration for twenty-five-plus centuries says, "Hi. Welcome to Walmart."—well, you might want to show just a little bit more reverence, OK?

Now, for those of you who may be a bit taken aback by thinking you know what Buddha looks like, that you've seen statues of him or paintings of him a zillion times in Chinese or Japanese restaurants, and as far as your concerned he doesn't look a thing like the greeter at your particular Walmart, well, have no fear—all is still right with the universe. And, you're right. Buddha does look like what you think he looks like.

But he's also female. Gay. Black. Asian. Caucasian. Named "Bubba." Drives an eighteen-wheeler. Has gotten a ticket for speeding. Is seven feet tall. Is three years old. Has warts. Eats garlic. Loves cats. Hates dogs. Does two-step country dancing. Is none of the above. Is all of the above.

And is still a greeter at Walmart. Life's simple sometimes.

Now, if you were to become so bold, so shameless, (so amused?) as to actually ask your friendly local Walmart Buddha/greeter why it is that (s)he, so to speak, "hides his or her Buddha nature under a basket" by, among other things, acting as a humble greeter at a mass-merchandising department store, well, you might not get the sunshine-and-goodness, love-thy-neighbor answer you expect.

Not by a long shot. In fact, your new "spiritual buddy" just might call security and have them unceremoniously bundle and eighty-six your philosophical, Buddha-inquiring self into the great outdoors, toot sweet.

That is, of course, unless you're into Zen and therefore already know that, son of a gun, Kris is right, you know—Buddha **is** a greeter at Walmart, and as such, I don't need to mention that fact to him or her. In fact, as I mentioned, this book takes that approach: using aspects of everyday life to help you deepen your understanding and/or appreciation of Zen. If I manage to help you with that, my job is done here.

As you read, you'll notice that I may approach one or more of the "lessons" in this book from one or more angles. That is, different chapters may convey the same lesson, but from different perspectives.

That's intentional.

How often have you looked at a piece of art, for example, from one perspective, then changed to a new perspective and perceived the art in a totally new way? The same concept applies here, but it is me rather than you who is supplying the various perspectives.

So, now that I've let the cat out of the bag about the fact that the guy putting yellow smiley-face stickers on your kids is Buddha, I hope you'll stick around for the rest of the book and what I (and my publisher) hope will be an interesting and maybe even thought-provoking experience of Zen. I also hope you'll have fun.

Hey—where else are you likely to see venerated, thousand-year-old Zen stories cheek-by-jowl with a greeter at the "low prices" center of the universe?

Welcome to Walmart. Welcome to Zen.

The Chrysalis of Time

I'm curious—by a show of hands, how many of you reading this book have realized how much we have in common with caterpillars and butterflies?

I see. Not too many.

We do, actually. Let's just look at the basic science. Sentient beings, as a start. Life. Air breathers. DNA and RNA. Earth atmosphere-centric. Heck, the list goes on and on.

But few of us take the time to realize that a jaw-dropping lesson of Zen can be conveyed by a butterfly. Lesson? Well, you're right, my bad. I meant to say, *lessons*. Let's say the "butterfly" has just left the chrysalis. Logical questions might include:

- Where did the caterpillar go?
- Did the caterpillar die?
- Where did the butterfly come from?
- How does the caterpillar change into a butterfly?

Do you see the pattern here? It is as plain as the pattern on a butterfly's wings: Zen.

To begin with, what was formerly known as "caterpillar" stays at the position of caterpillar. And what is latterly known as "butterfly" stays at the position of butterfly. A caterpillar doesn't "become" a butterfly any more than day "becomes" night.

Need proof? Watch a time-lapse movie of a caterpillar-butterfly. At no point will you ever see the caterpillar "come" or "go" anywhere.

Instead, you'll see the seamless, timeless *thus*. Reality.

The Wild Geese Know

One night, Henry, who was studying Buddhism with Bob, was walking through a meadow when they saw some wild geese in flight.

Bob asked, "What is that?" and Henry answered, "Wild geese."

Bob then asked, "Where did they go?" and Henry's answer was, "They flew away."

Bob gave Henry's nose a hard twist causing Henry to howl in pain.

Bob said, "Where could they have gone?"

This was the moment when Bob *saw*.

Zen Do

The world around us operates at a level which those folks who are not awake simply can't deal with. These same folks believe they know the world by knowing its names.

See; and if you must speak, and you speak English and want those around you to relate to what you're looking at; and if that which you are looking at resembles that which people for millennia have pointed to when making the "butterfly" vocalization, then you're good to go. Look. Say "butterfly."

Just don't conflate *thus*, and the vocalization, and the object (the butterfly), and the idea of the object.

Then what is it, I hear you ask?

It—is as timeless and nameless as … a butterfly.

The Crunch of a Fine Banana

I like bananas. You'll almost always find a bunch of organic bananas on my kitchen counter. Often, they're sitting next to a stack of yet-to-be-read magazines, which is fortunate for this chapter.

For example (from a magazine I actually did read), there was an article in an issue of *Time* entitled "Madman in the Kitchen." The article profiled an English chef named Heston Blumenthal, who was named "Best in the World" by *Restaurant* magazine, and whose restaurant, The Fat Duck, has been awarded three coveted stars by the venerable *Michelin Guide**.

For example, here, in his own words, is Heston Blumenthal's recipe for a staple on many American dinner tables: Spaghetti Bolognese (good old spaghetti with meat sauce.)

"As you might expect from a classic of the Italian kitchen, this involves no special equipment, just a long, slow simmer to allow the flavors to combine. However, I've added in a few things to boost those

* Not that you asked, but Gordon Ramsay is my favorite chef on Planet Earth. I'd watch that man boil water. Tea, Gordon?

flavors. Caramelizing onions with star anise produces vibrant flavor compounds that really enhance the meaty notes of the sauce, and the oaky quality of the chardonnay complements the sherry vinegar in the tomato compote. Finishing the compote on a high heat captures something of the fried character I enjoyed at Trattoria della Gigina. The use of milk might seem strange but it's a standard part of many Italian ragù recipes: as it cooks, the proteins and sugars in milk react to give extra flavor and body."

Milk in spaghetti? A "fried character"? "Caramelizing onions with star anise"? "Oaky spaghetti"?

But part of you wants to taste it, right? To be sure, an interesting (and taste-tempting) approach. Especially when you consider that Mr. Blumenthal was a photocopier salesman just a few years ago.

Maybe that ability to take risks (salesman to master chef) is what got him where he is today. The *Time* article detailed how one part of Mr. Blumenthal's well-deserved reputation for fine repast comes from his willingness to purposely combine new (or at least unique) food combinations of various tastes and textures such as the one we just read.

That got me thinking about how much of the world we miss by not being *mindful.*

We become programmed (or program ourselves) about things like, well, food—such as spaghetti or a how a common, everyday banana tastes. How a banana feels to your senses. How a banana looks. And the sound a banana makes when you peel it and eat it.

How often do we eat a banana **without** ever having mindfully experienced reality?

Master It Faster

A martial arts student went to his teacher and said earnestly, "I am devoted to studying your martial system. How long will it take me to master it."

The teacher's reply was casual, "Ten years." Impatiently, the student answered, "But I want to master it faster than that. I will work very hard. I will practice everyday, ten or more hours a day if I have to. How long will it take then?"

The teacher thought for a moment, "20 years."

Zen Do

Ask yourself, inside your kitchen or outside, how much of life are you missing right now because, like the student in our story above, you work(ed) very hard at mastering how life should be just-this-way and just-so.

Yet the life we can live, when done mindfully, is so very much richer than our stereotypes, so much more layered and subtle than our fixed definitions.

With awareness, with focus, with mindfulness every single occurrence is, by definition, new, unique and chock-full of new experiences, new opportunities to learn and experience.

So it is that each banana, each encounter with a person, each bowl of spaghetti is a whole new set of experiences which lay waste to preconceptions.

That's why (and how) our celebrity chef earns stars in the *Michelin Guide*—he's not bound by what combinations of tastes, textures, or colors are "supposed" to "go together."

For me, bananas do make a noise when I peel and eat them. That's my experience and my Zen.

Ask yourself, inside your kitchen or outside, how much of life, of reality, of Zen, are you missing—right here, right now—because you failed to notice, say, the crunch of a fine banana.

Time for you to get *cooking*.

Ginger Rogers and the Zen of Cruise Liners

For many people, trying to navigate the workday is a tough task. Let's see if any of this sounds familiar to you: dog-eat-dog politics, cutthroat markets, management by emotion, the Peter Principle, and the minefields of road rage, parking-lot traffic, and not enough hours in the day.

Now imagine something a bit ... different. In fact, I will give you two examples of a different sort of "work environment."

To begin with, imagine that in order to park your car in your assigned parking space at work, you had to:

- Back your car in. (Hey, I didn't say they all had to be hard...)
- Between other cars of the same size that, if you hit one, may, well, sink.
- All the cars have upwards of 3,000 people in them.
- You don't have brakes.
- The pavement you're parking on, well, moves (you see, it's the ocean, to be precise, with shoals, a shifting sandy bottom, currents, winds, tides, crazy lighting, and crazy boat drivers zipping around).

- Your car now weighs 110,000 tons.
- And your car isn't a car ... it's a cruise liner.

Sound nuts? Well, believe it or not, this sort of thing happens several times a day. And the folks "parking" these "cars" get it 100% right 100% of the time despite the fact that:

- Every ship handles a bit different.
- Much of what happens in parking and piloting these behemoths takes place backward, with very little room for error.
- It takes serious experience to stop a 110,000-ton ship on a dime (... yard ... acre ...)
- There are many people talking around these folks at the same time they're trying to do their job.
- There's the weather and the sea. One of these is tough to deal with. Both, especially when both are in bad moods, require unbelievable focus.
- You can't actually handle every control, tool, and aspect of the task at hand by yourself. You have to order other people to do what you want them to do and count on them doing it right ... every time.
- Parking is extra tough when the front or rear "fender" of your "car" is, say, 300 feet away.

They say Ginger Rogers did everything Fred Astaire did—but backward and in high heels. Watch any of their movies closely and you will see why doing so is astonishingly difficult—and how she made it all seem effortless. I mean, she smiled the whole time!

These are clear examples of Zen at work. Dancing or parking a cruise liner with attention to detail. Focus. Supreme awareness. *Mindfulness.*

Zen Wizardry: Eating and Drinking

A war was about to start between two lords in Japan. The object in dispute was a valley, rich in soil, rivers, minerals, and timber.

The two lords agreed that rather than an all out battle, they would each choose only one of their finest swordsman to represent them. Ownership of the land would be determined by that two person fight.

The man selected by the Lord of the East was not sure he was capable of defeating the swordsman for the Lord of the West. The swordsman's fear was not of death, but of the shame his defeat would shower on his family, his name, and his Lord.

"Please instruct me," he asked his Zen teacher.

"I have taught you all I know," his teacher said.

"Then what thoughts should I take into combat?" the warrior asked.

"No thoughts. Take the mind of the frog," his teacher commanded.

"I do not understand," the warrior said.

"Watch carefully and learn," said the teacher, leading the swordsman to a pond where a large frog sat stone still on the bank. In time, a large blue-green fly flitted by and with no movement save a coiled spring, the frog sprung forward and ate the fly.

"Tomorrow, in combat, be the frog. Do not think. Be. Empty your mind. Meditate from tonight until the morrow's dawn on the frog's single-mindedness, its focus. When the moment of opportunity arises—be your sword."

For the rest of his life, the swordsman was revered for his faultless performance in that battle. And ever-after, that swordsman wore the emblem of the frog on his sword, armor, saddle, and even on his family's coat of arms.

Zen Do

Zen is the task at hand, period. Dancing. Or piloting a cruise liner. Zen is attention, awareness, focus. Mindfulness.

Not thinking <u>about</u> the task at hand—simply doing what needs to be done, right here, right now. If your monkey mind wants to wander (which it usually does, especially for those new to Zen practice), the solution to this problem is as simple as a Ginger Rogers two-step: simply return your attention to the task at hand—time after time after time. That's it.

Is it hard work to keep dragging your mind back to the task at hand? You bet! But it is important work for those who wish to be awake. (Besides, it's easier than dancing backward.)

If all you master is the simple art of bringing your mind back to here and now every time it wants to wander off to someplace else, I'm confident you could park a cruise liner, no sweat.

Arguably, one of the simplest, most critical, deep, and most obvious lessons of Zen is that: be here and now. Over and over and over again, microsecond by microsecond.

Whether she knew it as such or not, without Zen, Ginger Rogers could not have danced a step forward or backward.

Grab a movie of hers and watch her dance. Whatever you call it, what you will see is a Zen master at work. Can you say the same thing about your attention to reality? Your work? Your Zen?

Care to dance?

The Junk Drawer

If you're like me, you have a drawer, usually in the kitchen that is almost universally referred to as the junk drawer.

Inside this drawer are all manner of householder flotsam and jetsam—old keys (no one knows which locks these fit, but it always seems important to keep them) ... pencils (sans erasers but often with an amazing array of teeth marks) ... pens (which, as a rule, have a blob of indescribable gunk on the ball point, guaranteeing a large, inky blotch at the start of the first word you attempt to write) ... assorted screwdrivers (which, when you need them, are always the wrong size or shape) ... combination locks (no one remembers the combination, but maybe one day someone will) ... an old remote control (to a TV you no longer own) ... the plastic things that clip onto the twisted-up end of the wrapper on a loaf of bread ... twist ties from other items wrapped in plastic ... expired library cards ... ticket stubs from a movie you saw last spring ... all manner of things—and all usually resting on a bedding of business cards that lines the bottom of the drawer.

However, for most folks, there is more to the contents of a junk drawer than, well, junk. For these people, the items in a typical junk drawer hold messages, meanings, thoughts, ideas, definitions, or emotions (or some combination of these) that supersede the physical nature of any particular item.

And while almost everyone has a junk drawer, few people realize that it serves another purpose: it's an excellent place for studying Zen.

Let's look at a couple of examples to support that idea.

Let's say, as I mentioned above, that this particular junk drawer contains movie ticket stubs, and that these particular stubs are from a movie titled *Winged Migration* (a movie whose whole story line, and sparse narration, is focused on—yep, you guessed it—bird migration). Well, that's what many people would think about if they saw a pair of *Winged Migration* ticket stubs in a drawer: ticket stubs from a movie about birds. So where's the insight there? Zen where?

But imagine this: perhaps for you, these ticket stubs hold meaning far beyond flights of Canada geese and other winged critters. For you, these tickets are a link to, say, an epiphany about nature that you experienced while watching the movie. And, these ticket stubs also remind you of the impact, the speechlessness, the clarity of understanding that often accompanies such an epiphany. For you, these ticket stubs are the marker, the index, the bond, if you will, to those feelings and those ideas, and you keep the ticket stubs to somehow hold on to the idea of the epiphany.

Let's take another example.

Perhaps one of the business cards on the bottom of your junk drawer is from the manager of the theater where you saw *Winged Migration*. And perhaps you keep her business card to remind you of the fender bender your car suffered in the theater's parking lot while you were watching the movie inside—and the anger and frustration you felt upon seeing the damage done to your car.

So you keep her business card as a reminder of just how careful one needs to be in a parking lot. Or, as a prompt to remind yourself to always park away from other people's cars. Or, because, well, you never know when you'll need to talk to the theater manager again—provided, of course, that you go to that particular theater again, and provided she is still managing that theater, and provided you actually have a reason to talk to her, and ... well, you get the idea.

But again, to you, her business card is more than just a business card—it's a link to a package of ideas and emotions, and it's not "junk."

Or is it?

The Card

A fabulously wealthy cattle rancher in Texas was beset by calamities.

In a matter of just a few months he lost his beautiful (pain-in-the-neck) trophy wife to another man, his 27,000 square foot mansion to fire, his bank accounts and businesses to a thieving accountant—and his freedom for driving his pickup truck through the glass doors of the county court house, which promptly burned to the ground.

In prison, one of the jailers befriended the rancher, and over time noticed something about the man's behavior.

He seemed quite happy.

"Listen here. Are you in your right mind, mister?" asked the jailer. "Why do you smile, and laugh, and seem to pass each day so damn peaceably?"

"That's simple," chuckled the rancher. "Absolutely nothing left to lose."

Zen Do

Search your "junk drawers"—the one in your house *and* the one in your mind—and see which items you find and which you can dispose of. Attachment, the Buddha said, is suffering.

Remember that in Zen, we're always looking for what we can eliminate, what we can throw out, and we're always looking for ways to see what it is that blocks us from seeing *what is* because of what we think something *says* or what we *think* something is.

As almost any Zen teacher will tell you, "Whatever you think, that is your delusion."

You may well discover that by reading and reviewing some of the "labels" you have consciously or unconsciously placed on items in your physical or mental junk drawer, you'll also realize that those labels are hiding, well, *junk,* which deserves to be thrown out.

And perhaps you'll also see that you've been unable to throw some of these things out because you confused the label with the thing.

See that and you may well find a new state of mind: one that is spare, clean, and free of junk—and with nothing left to lose.

Zen as Sweet as Honey

Bees go about their work with a focus on the moment, so in this respect they have much to teach anyone interested in spending more time in the here and now and less time multitasking their life away.

Sit for a moment and see a mental picture of bees working in a hive.

Do you think they are spending ANY time wondering about what is going to happen next week, what happened last week, or even what is going to happen two seconds from now?

No—nor should you.

There It Is!

Joni was studying with Rebecca, a teacher at the Zen School in Phoenix.

One day Joni encountered Rebecca crossing the school's courtyard. Joni said, "Teacher, what is the essential teaching of Buddhism?"

Rebecca never broke stride as she looked straight ahead and walked past her student. Suddenly, Rebecca stopped and called out, "JONI!"

Joni instantly responded, "Yes?"

Rebecca said, "There it is!"

Zen Do

The noisy and demanding world you live in wants your attention. But that attention is yours—to give or reclaim as you wish. No one owns it but you. What is the key to reclaiming it?

Mindfulness. Focus. You, busy as a bee, just being.

Honey, anyone?

Fourth Down and Nirvana to Go

We all know people who fit this profile:

- An ex-"Big Person on Campus." As in, he was, say, the former captain of the football team, or class president. Or, perhaps she was head cheerleader, or class treasurer. Or, there was a picture of the two of them in the senior yearbook with the caption "Most Desirable."
- He or she always seems to be talking in terms of "Remember when …"
- He or she is not happy with "the way things are today" and constantly seems to be saying that, well, everything was easier, or better, or simpler, or … *something* … "back then."
- He or she is always planning (more typically, talking about planning) a "comeback" or "big move," a rather vaguely detailed construct that will propel him or her "back on top" where (s)he "belongs."
- He or she isn't a very pleasant person to be around for most people. There are clear indications of anger, acrimony, and disappointment

earmarking his or her personality. And these become *very* visible indeed, after a couple of stiff drinks.*

These folks are carrying around a very rigid view and definition of the world and a very fixed idea of where they see themselves (and everyone else) in that world. Whether or not that reflects *reality* is another issue—and my point here.

Big Man?

Legend tells us the story of two men, the most famous debaters on Zen and Buddhism in all the world.

Each of these debaters traveled with a posse of supporters who cheered their speaker on, and who catered to their every whim, constantly stroking the speaker's ego and treating them like princes.

Word had been circulating that these two gentlemen were to face each other in a five-day long debate in San Francisco. Student and teachers of Zen and Buddhism flocked from all across the globe to hear these men.

Once the competition started, a pattern emerged: first one debater would carry the day, then the next day the other would. At the end of four days, everyone thought the debate so far was a tie.

Each debater's posse wore themselves to a frazzle stroking their patron's ego.

On the fifth night of the debate, the two adversaries brought forth their very best arguments and styles. Each verbally thrust, cut, and parried the arguments of their foe. And after each successful verbal strike, each debater would puff himself up and parade the room to the cheers of his posse and other supporters.

*Or their inhibition remover of choice.

This was all well and good—until a huge explosion ripped the debate hall causing all manner of disturbance, knocking over chairs and tables, and people too. The walls, ceiling and floor were covered in an ungodly mess.

Once order had been returned to the room, it was discovered that the debaters themselves—had swelled-up so much they exploded.

Zen Do

Insisting that you have a "place," or demanding in one form or another that other people treat you as if you have/had a place, is an addiction symptom of the worst drug in history: ego.

Ego revels in creating models that are patently inaccurate and have zero ability to represent reality. But—to those who are not awake, *boy, are ego's models fun!*

Moreover, when it's not building phantom reflections of nonexistent worlds, conditions, or situations, ego keeps you by its side by wrapping you in layers of emotional fog (envy, greed, suspicion, and pride, for a start) about those ideas, and uses this fog to reinforce your "need" for both the models and fog … and the models and the fog … and the models and the fog … and the whole sick pattern builds on itself ad nauseam.

Ego drives the emotions to reinforce the model, and vice versa, and you find yourself espousing a belief in some view of your past, for example, that feels real, even justified. And is anything but.

Perhaps even more insidious, ego leads you to think that as good as that model of you and the "good ol' days" may be (the ego-built phantom reflection), *just you wait*—tomorrow will be even better!

Then as folks afflicted with this condition age, the whole phantom house of cards starts to fall down, slowly at first, one card at a time. ("Hmmm ... my knee's playing hell with me. Maybe I can't run for a touchdown as fast as I used to. Bah, I can still run faster than those others—it'll be fast enough.") But it isn't.

Then another card falls (perhaps you have to start reminding people how good you were—and they not only don't seem to remember, but worse yet, they just don't seem to care ...), and another card, and another.

And then you see them—perhaps physically, perhaps spiritually, or perhaps emotionally—twisted, angry, resentful, and poisoned. Wrapped, hardened, and walking around to save funeral expenses. And self-hatred is the ego's last redoubt.

The lesson is: here and now. Here and now, in Zen, you *see* that you couldn't be the person you were, even if you wanted to—that was then and this is now. This issue isn't time: it's you, a condition of reality here and now.

For those who are truly awake to the moment, there are no time-outs, no substitutions, and no room for ego. There's just you—and your true unwritten nature is greater than that of any one person or "place," concept of person or place, or memory of the same.

Way to go, champ!

A Few Choice Words on Religion

What does Zen have to do with religion?

Beats me, but I get asked about Zen from Catholics, Mormons, Jews, and Reform Druids,* so I'd better buckle down and write a chapter on the topic.

Shaking Zen

Janelle, a Zen student, asked her teacher, Chris, "What is the essence of Zen?"

Chris came from behind his desk, grabbed Janelle by the shirt sleeves, shook her hard several times, and then shoved her away.

Janelle stood there blinking.

Vince, another student standing nearby asked Janelle, "Well? Why don't you make a deep bow?"

A smile slid across Janelle's lips as she gained enlightenment and bowed deeply.

* They say reform druids only pray at bushes and potted palms, not at full-on trees...

Zen Do

Zen is your experience and reality, pure and simple, and is so without the need for an overlay of something as divisive as "religion."

It's that simple.

We're done here.

Alan Watts Wears Funny Glasses

As I mentioned earlier, to a large extent I was raised on the Zen of Alan Watts. My mother set me on the Watts path at a tender age, and that was a good thing—it set my dharma wheel to spinning when I didn't even know I had one. His work still has a profound impact on me today, all these years later.

Yet whether it is Alan Watts—or anyone else—a key understanding must be that no one has "All The Answers." When you reflect on that for a moment, two of the reasons why that is become obvious: reality may be *thus* but our enlightenment happens little by little, and by whose authority?

No matter who they are or were—Buddha, Alan Watts, Kris Neely, or the crazy guy walking up and down Market Street in San Francisco carrying a sign that really does read, "The end is near! Ask me how and why!*"—the "teacher's" views were created in the furnace of his or her own teachings, prejudices, genetics, environment, upbringing, delusion, and sense of self (or lack of same).**

* Seriously, there really is such a guy!

**Or it could just be an effect of the weather on their planet. Or it could just be tight Jockey shorts.

Every Little Bit Helps

Teri, a Zen teacher, and Steve, one of her students, were returning late at night along a narrow and sheer path to their mountaintop school.

As they walked, a brutal winter storm overtook them. To stop, meant death by exposure. Going on, meant the risk of a deadly fall from one of the slippery rocks and crags which lined their way.

They had no choice but to go forward. But between the rain, the howling wind, the dark clouds, and the inky black night, it had become almost impossible to clearly see the way forward. Their only hope lay in trying to navigate by the brief flashes of lightning which randomly light-up the night and their trail.

So Teri and Steve crept forward with each flash. In between flashes, they huddled together, trying to make out and memorize the path ahead.

Their progress was slow. Finally, they made it to the school.

Warming themselves by the stove in the school's kitchen, Steve confessed to Teri, "What scared me the most out there wasn't the elements—it was the idea of dying without attaining enlightenment."

With a wry smile, Teri said, "Enlightenment is not the sun that shines all day, but the lightening that gives only quick glimpses allowing us to navigate from one troubled place in our lives to another."

"Is that true for you too, Teacher?" asked Steve.

"It is true for most of us," said Teri.

Zen Do

To be sure, Alan Watts pointed the way to new insights about myself, Zen, and Buddhism. His words (and those of my Mom) first lit the path of Zen for me.

But their words are not the only source of illumination for me as I move along the Middle Way. To fixate on their teachings (or on anyone's teachings) might actually strand me on the path to enlightenment not illuminate it.

From the first day of my Zen studies to now, I've seen that the words of anyone, even someone as respected as Alan Watts, would be just some words among many which might trigger a flash of enlightenment in me.

Early on I saw that each flash, regardless of its source and time, (read: regardless of its source/author and regardless of the duration between flashes) helps me see the way ahead—one glimpse at a time.

And by extension, each flash is also a bright and vivid reminder of one of the Buddha's most profound teachings: question authority. All authority, that of The Buddha, my Mom's, Alan Watts'—anyone's.

So as I navigate along my path, I honor my old teacher; by finding a picture of him on which to draw funny glasses.

Ah. Lightening.

And Just *Who* Said You Could Take Your Next Breath?

I just read an email. In it, I learned that a coworker's body has been found in an accicental airplane crash in the Alps. The email goes on to say that my coworker leaves behind a wife, two teenage children, and a baby girl.

Daily life works like that: One moment a person is a worker, father, son, dad, lover, colleague, and uncle. And the next moment ... The Japanese have a saying: "One inch forward and all is black."

So—let's move that one inch forward. Here's what I want you to do ...

Die.

Right now, right where you are. Die.

And let's be clear here: what I'm asking for is not a Hallmark card/ romantic death surrounded by loving family, flowers, peaceful music, and a bright white light leading you on to Grandma's smiling face, apple pie, and a Chicago Cubs team that can win the World Series.*

Nope—just dead. Late. Snuffed. Deceased. Lifeless. Gone. Toast. Departed. Popped. Pegged out. Chased in. Cashed out. Road kill.

*Yeah, right! *Oh, wait—they DID!*

Is ex-animate. Bit the shit. Modeling a pine overcoat. Gathering the asphalt. Vampire in training. Is "Tango Uniform." Assumed room temperature. Kicked the bucket. Answered the final summons. Hopped on the last rattler. At the ghost talent audition. Achieved negative patient care outcome. Picking turnips with a stepladder. Hitched a ride in the meat wagon. Checked in at the Morgue Motel. Getting one's mail delivered by moles. Gone to sing with the choir invisible. The latest addition to the zombie conga line.

Now—having gotten that straight, think about being dead for a few minutes. Think about your family, work, your hobbies and friends, your worries and concerns. All now someone else's concerns—if even that.

Now ... see the clarity that being dead offers?

Issues and items you thought "important" now look trivial. Worries and attitudes toward events and people may be completely changed, possibly reversed.

And wouldn't you give anything—*anything*—for one more kiss from your son, daughter, husband, wife, mom, or dad?

Yeah, it's a bitch being worm chow—but it can be an enlightened one at that. I'll explain more in a minute.

Dying to Wake Up

A Zen monk embarked on a journey to find both the Buddha and enlightenment.

He traveled far and wide, year after year. His trek took him to the land where Buddha was said to live. Crossing a river in this country, the monk looked upstream and noticed something floating toward him.

As it got closer, he realized that it was the corpse of a person.

When it drifted so close that the monk could almost touch the bloated, disgusting thing, he suddenly recognized the dead body—it was his own!

The realization came as a crashing thunderbolt to his mind. He lost all control and wailed and cried, screaming as if mad, tearing his hair and lamenting the pitiful sight of himself, still and lifeless, dead and gone, drifting along the river's currents.

That moment was the beginning of his liberation.

Zen Do

The next time you sit zazen—don't take your next breath for granted.

Not only see, but *see* **each** breath. *See* that each breath is both life and death in one small, compact form. See that in just the same way that you can't only breathe in or only breathe out, you also can't have only living without dying.

In that instant, perhaps like a thunderbolt to your mind, you'll *see* yourself "alive" and "dead" and also *see* that that which makes the living possible and the dying necessary was never, could never, be born and so it cannot "die." *

In addition, *see* how so many things in the universe make your very breathing possible: oxygen, plants, trees, the sun, nitrogen, carbon dioxide, rain, wind, air pressure, cellular

*For the purposes of this chapter, let's leave the whole religion/heaven/hell thing to one side, OK? Great, now back to the story ...

exchange, water ... the list goes on and on. In fact—start following the chain of your breath and you're likely to find ... everything. And in finding it all, you'll see yet again that while your physical body may "die" (whatever that is), you—the real you that existed before your mother's and father's mothers and fathers were born—always has and always will exist, and can and could never die.

Zen makes it possible to see and attain this. When you do, you'll also see that this day—any day—is a good day to die.

See you on the conga line!

The Awesome Majesty of Ashes

Go into any seat of power or social hierarchy (hereafter known as an "Important Place") and you'll find yourself face-to-face with a set, a stage, an artifice of some type designed to inform you that equally "Important Things" happen there.

You're also likely to discover "Important People" playing equally (or, in their minds, more) "Important Roles."

And finally, you'll also learn that only in such an "Important Place," and only with these "Important People" doing these "Important Roles and Things," could anything really—you guessed it—"Important" ever get done.

Examples of these "Important Places" include churches, courts, banks, schools, law offices, doctors' offices, city, state, and national government offices, and yes, even Zen temples. And some folks believe that without the "Important Places," how could the "Important Work" ever get done?

And that's an "Important Question."

Well, not really, but I was on a roll. The reality is that it's too bad that this everything-must-occur-on-its-appointed-stage approach to life permeates so much of our daily lives. Not only is it largely a colossal waste of time, energy, and money in many cases, it also obscures the beauty of a key aspect of Zen: that wherever you might be, *that* is your church, your office, or your monastery, and there is no need for a stage.

Life is real, life is the stage, and there's no need for, or room for, a rehearsal hall. They may make rehearsals all that much better, but in Zen we see that life is lived, not rehearsed.

Gaining that perspective took me awhile and was due in no small part to my finally coming to appreciate ... the awesome majesty of ashes. And the splendor of mold, the magnificence of trash, and the art and glory of rust.

Somehow I suspect you'd like an explanation of that.

Polishing My Zen

A Zen master encountered a student engaged in deep meditation, seated in a garden.

The master asked what he was doing, and the student replied that he was meditating in order to achieve Buddhahood.

As he listened, the master noticed a clay tablet close by and began polishing it.

When the student asked about this seemingly strange behavior, the Zen master said, "I'm polishing the clay tablet to form a mirror."

The student asked how polishing a clay tablet could possibly form a mirror, to which the Zen master replied, "How can sitting in meditation form a Buddha?"

Zen Do

Like all great Zen stories, this one operates on many levels and offers doors to many levels of Zen. Here's the level I'm focused on in this chapter: place, form, dress, timing, location, setting, and rituals, have little (to no) value in Zen. They are simply means to an end—if you need them as such.

Zen, reality, and truth are whenever and wherever you are. Right here, right now, regardless of place or time.

A moldy piece of wood, a dirty ashtray, a weedy lot, or the blood and gore of war? Reflect what you see, attain the reality of that moment. Do not be led astray by titles, names, locations, or concepts. Looking for a cathedral? Reality is your cathedral.

Just see what you see as you see it, and don't become attached to what you see or wish the scene had better lighting or better actors. It is what it is—just so, and it doesn't need a "theater."

If you can't find Zen when looking into a dirty ashtray, how do ever expect to find it on the stage of a Zen temple? And if you can't find Zen in yourself, which actor do you suppose knows *your* part and *your* lines?

If you're waiting for that actor to appear, you might as well start polishing your own clay tablet.

That sounds like "Important Work" to me.

Bam, Slug, and Wham-o Your Way to Enlightenment

In traveling around the world, I'm constantly amazed at what people think they *know*.

I don't know why this should surprise me—history is replete with, and some might say composed of, examples (or/and consequences) of what people *thought* they knew:

- "The world is flat!"
- "Earth is the center of the universe!"
- "Man will never fly!"
- "There are weapons of mass destruction in Iraq!"
- "No one will ever run a mile in less than four minutes!"
- "Zen is ...."

Yep—there's a whole lot of knowin' going on there. And think about it for a second—how many times a month do you start a sentence or a thought with, "I know ..."

The trick about *knowing something* is that time after time you come to find that what you thought you knew ... changed.

- "The world is round!"
- "Earth is not the center of the universe!"
- "Man Flies to Moon!"
- "There are NO WMDs in Iraq!"
- "New World Record for Mile: 3:43.13!"
- "Zen is (anything that follows those two words)."

A key aspect of Buddhism and Zen is *not* knowing. To try to know something means that you can define whatever it *is*. And no one has even been able to do that. Zen students are constantly prodded by Zen teachers who say something along the lines of, "One thought, or one sound, and heaven and earth are ripped apart."

In the Zen dharma I follow, students are admonished to "Don't *know*. Only go straight!*" **especially** when someone wants to "know" something—like what Zen is. Yes, I have a view, my view, of what Zen is, but that's my view, not something I *know*.

Yet it's as plain as the nose on my face ...

OUCH!!! Did You Say Insight?

A Zen student who had studied with many masters wished to demonstrate his attainment to his latest instructor.

As his teacher sat listening and smoking a bamboo pipe, the student said, "The mind, Buddha, and sentient beings, after all, do not exist. The true nature of phenomena is emptiness. There is no realization, no delusion, no sage, and no mediocrity. There is no giving and nothing to be received."

The teacher listened to this dogma and, moving suddenly, struck the student hard across the bridge of the student's nose with the pipe, saying, "If nothing exists, where did this anger come from?"

* With a respectful bow to Seung Sahn.

Zen Do

So—what do you think you know?

Reality has a way of taking such well-documented "knowledge" and hitting us right across the nose as a way of bringing us out of our dream world and smack-dab-a-do-ya back to *reality*: here and now.

And, as is so often the case, it hurts when this happens. Some folks even spend time asking why bad things like this or that happen to "good people." Or questioning what *they* did to get slammed by events, or KO'ed by circumstances, or whammed into a new way of seeing daily events by painful developments in their lives. And in such a state, many people will look for an authority ... a testament ... a model ... a vision ... a dream ... a belief ... or just a story to help them cope with their pain.

What there is, is *reality*. And the more time you spend *seeing* it and not "knowing" it—to that degree, your life lessons will be less painful.

Buddha said, in essence, desire is pain. Wanting things to be the way you *know* them to be is desire. Game, set, match: pain wins.

Ding! There's the bell for right here and right now: come out fighting!

A Butterfly on Battery Street

Sometime back, I was walking along Market Street in San Francisco, enjoying the sights, sounds, and smells of the City by the Bay, when I had occasion to turn left onto Battery Street.

Watching my step along a somewhat treacherous section of sidewalk, I noticed what appeared to be a dead butterfly lying on the ground. In an instant, my mind seemed to show me an impossibly fast time-lapse movie that connected this particular butterfly to every occurrence, definition, image, lesson, speech, emotion, and sense memory I have for "butterfly," stretching from that moment back in time to my first memories of butterflies, in grade school.

I also think the butterfly on Battery Street was a powerful Zen lesson.

We program our minds layer by layer and memory by memory. We recognize the butterfly on Battery Street because we've seen images of things we were told were "butterflies." We then connect those images to other images of "butterflies" as we grow. We never really question why the tag "butterfly" applies to so many of these flying creatures; we see an image, compare it to images in our memory, and get a hit on "butterfly."

We also learn the emotions of butterflies as we grow older. I don't mean that we learn love, hate, and other emotions *from* butterflies; rather, we learn what emotions we are expected to display *about* butterflies. For example, one emotion of this type can be summed up in a single word, "Aww!"

We also learn that butterflies are supposed to be admired, treated delicately, revered as "cute, harmless, and beautiful creations," and we're taught that females of our species have a special fondness for both sexes of their species. We learn that men of our species are not supposed to be too crazy about any sexes of their species.

We're taught that butterflies, as delicate as they seem, are iron-lunged warriors of the sky who migrate from Canada to Mexico.* And they do so on what can only be called gossamer wings. We learn that our friends the butterflies have been migrating in that way for centuries, despite the rise of humans and our buildings, airplanes, pollutants, and lack of true understanding of the everyday needs of butterflies.

Ironically, considering all the thinking, emoting, and studies done on/about butterflies, there seems to be little empirical data to suggest that butterflies ever actually take notice of us at all—a Zen lesson of tremendous impact for such a delicate creature, but not the only one.

Not Dead Yet

Elizabeth asked Zen teacher Greg, "What happens to a man of enlightenment after death?"

"How should I know?" replied Greg.

"Because you are a Zen master," answered Elizabeth.

"Yes ma'am," said Greg, "but not a dead one."

*How many humans have ever even driven that far, much less walked—much less *flew!*

Zen Do

Robert Lynd said, "In order to see birds, it is necessary to become part of the silence."

That silence demands *seeing*, not listening to the speculative chattering of our inner Monkey Mind.

It also demands "not knowing."

What do I know about butterflies? I don't know, for I am not a butterfly.

I know the trivia I wrote about in the opening section of this chapter. But really, do I *know* any of that. They are feelings, impressions, ideas, emotions—even cliches.

I "know" exactly the same amount about butterflies as I do about lifeforms on Alpha Centauri. That is to say, nada.

I didn't see a dead butterfly on Battery Street in San Francisco. Instead, I *saw* a dead butterfly on Battery Street in San Francisco.

Colonel Mustard Did It in the Zendo

Remember the board game *Clue?* You know—"Colonel Mustard did it in the conservatory with the lead pipe!"

Then you also remember that the object of the game is threefold: to solve the mystery of who killed Mr. Boddy*, determine in which room of Mr. Boddy's estate the murder took place, and figure out the murderer's weapon of choice.

Players start the game by being uncertain as to who killed Mr. Boddy, collect and guess clues throughout the game, and end the game knowing who did what, where, and with what.

In that sense, *Clue* is much like how many people lead life: starting life in doubt and ending their life *certain* that they've divined all the clues and "figured it all out."

Tidy.

And just as fictional as "Colonel Mustard did it in the conservatory with the lead pipe!"

*Yeah ... apparently that's how the game maker spells it.

The Culprit Is … a Fish!

One day a Zen master and a friend were walking by a river.

"Look at the fish swimming about," said the master. "They are really enjoying themselves."

"You are not a fish," replied the friend, "so you can't be certain they're enjoying themselves."

"You are not me," said the master, "so how are you certain that I'm not certain the fish are enjoying themselves?"

Zen Do

There is a saying: "To be uncertain is uncomfortable. To be certain is ridiculous."

Zen teaches us that there is no certainty. There is, in fact, nothing that can be depended on, named, enumerated, promised, guaranteed, created, or destroyed. If you can think of it, from A to Z and beyond, *whatever it is you think of* is uncertain—because it doesn't really reflect reality, only an idea *about* reality.

There isn't what you think—there simply is. And it is *thus.*

We're done here, Colonel Mustard.

Mindfulness is Just a Pastry Away

Ms. Bharti Kirchner is the author of a book titled *Pastries: A Novel of Desserts and Discoveries*. This fascinating work tells the story of a baker named Sunya who travels to Japan in an attempt to get past her "baker's block"—essentially, the baker's equivalent of the more widely known "writer's block." In other words, Sunya's baking creativity was stalled.

Although all of Ms. Kirchner's book is a delight, much like its subject, one paragraph in particular struck me:

"I fill each rectangle with chocolate sauce, a bounty of thin apple slices, and whipped cream, thinking of nothing but what am I doing. Me and my pastry. It all comes down to that ... I can do this."

Quite a mindfulness lesson there, as this story will underscore.

Zen Pastries

Easily one of the most famous Zen stories of all time goes like this:

Zen student: "Master, I'm new to this monastery. Please instruct me in Zen."

Zen master: "Have you finished your breakfast?"

Zen student: "Yes."

Zen master: "Then clean your bowl."

At this, the student was enlightened.

Zen Do

Life never stops moving. Reality never stops moving. If you take even a billionth of a second to consider such thoughts, to think *about*, as it were, you will never be able to get the lost fraction of a second of reality back.

Moreover, since many of us are thinking about things like how much we don't like what we're doing at a given moment, or thinking about how we're being put upon to do this or that, or thinking about how we should really be getting paid better for doing this or that—basically thinking about things that have nothing to do with here and now and the work/reality at hand, we can clearly see how baker's block can occur: it isn't doing, it's thinking about doing.

Remember the paragraph from *Pastries* that we just read? I see it this way:

Doing: Fill.

Thought: ________. *If anything comes to mind, let it pass.*

Repeat.

Doing: Fill.

Thought: ________. *If anything comes to mind, let it pass.*

Repeat.

Doing: Fill.

Thought: ________. *If anything comes to mind, let it pass.*

Repeat.

Doing what needs to be done without clinging to thoughts; just letting thoughts pass and returning to work.

Mindful work—*ah, fresh-baked Zen!*

The Entire Known World—in a Dry Cleaning Bag

I went to the dry cleaner in my neighborhood the other day to pick up a shirt. The clerk dutifully hung a white business shirt, encased in a transparent dry cleaning bag, on a convenient laundry cart.

Just one problem: it wasn't my shirt. Don't ask me how I knew, I just knew—that shirt wasn't mine.

True, the bag had a tag with my name clearly emblazoned on it, to be sure—but it wasn't my shirt.

Wasting not a minute, the clerk whisked the not-my-shirt away and disappeared into a forest of dry cleaning. A few moments later, I saw the glow of a black light in the clothing forest. Then, following quickly, I heard a muffled "A-ha!"

The clerk reappeared with a dry cleaning bag that held a white business shirt.

I'll save you the stress* by saying yes, it was my shirt (even though the tag on *this* dry cleaning bag was labeled with someone else's name).

*And probably ruin the movie for some of you.

Yet how, I'm sure you're wondering, did the clerk know *this* was actually my shirt, if not my dry cleaning bag?

Exactly my question to the now-smiling clerk, who told me that she'd seen my name, written in fine, neat block-letter printing on the back of my shirt by using the black light. Apparently, some dry cleaners do that: they write the customer's name on a garment with a sort of pen whose "ink" is only visible via the illuminations of the aforementioned ultraviolet light.

Not knowing that explanation at the time, I naturally asked the clerk if anyone could "see" my name on the shirt, and she replied, "Not people, no. But bees can. They see ultraviolet light."

With that answer, this clerk had done more for, and to, me than find my shirt and demonstrate basic high school science. She helped me understand a key teaching of Zen.

I'll explain.

As children, we are taught that "blue" looks like, well, blue and "red" looks like, well, red, and so on. We store that information in that place in our minds where we keep other such "constants"—pounds and ounces, numbers, letters, etc.

From then on, the sound made by pronouncing the letter sequence "blue" will be what we enunciate when we observe what we were taught was blue.

OK, you say, so what? Blue is blue.

Well, blue may be something, but I'll tell you one thing: it ain't blue.

Why? The science alone would take hours to explain*, so let's start with these issues:

*If I knew it well enough to do so in sufficient detail.

- Blue-colorblind people don't see the same blue you and I see. These folks see a different gradation of the light spectrum—their experience, or view, if you will, of blue is way different from, say, yours. True, the sound "blue" (see also: label) is the same, but the *experience* is different.
- Still other people can't see, for most regular definitions, any colors at all—they only see black and white. These folks are born with only their black and white photoreceptors functional. So, like the previous group, these folks know that something called "blue" (and the sound/label) exists, but their experience of it is different from yours and mine.

On another tack, let's take a hypothetical case: imagine that somewhere in the world a child is being taught that the letter sequence "poteday" is equivalent to our letter sequence "blue." To this child, poteday is not the same as blue because (s)he has no point of reference for blue.

You could be playing a game with this child and ask him or her to pick up the blue ball, and be somewhat surprised when he or she didn't—after all, you might reason, *everyone* knows what blue is.

But the issue here isn't with the child—the issue is with the label. Despite the fact that this child speaks perfectly good English, (s)he simply didn't learn the label "blue." True, (s)he *sees* what (s)he calls poteday and what you call blue when looking at the ball, for example, and the end result (observe the round object that is illuminated with such-and-such frequencies of light), but the labels are different—and are also, in one sense, irrelevant, interfering, argumentative, and ultimately unnecessary.

Add in the additional fact that human eyes see only a tiny fraction of the electromagnetic spectrum (as we learned with the "the bees can see your name printed on your shirt, but you can't" lesson, above), and the point becomes manifest. Be they X-rays, infrared light, gamma rays, or "poteday," we each call the world into being based on the tools we have or are equipped with: eyes that see visible light, not ultraviolet, and so on.

Finally, "blue" really is an illusion of bad semantics. If I ask one hundred people to point out something blue, am I always going to get/see the same *shade* of blue? No—I'm likely to get/see navy blue, sky blue, and robin's egg blue, pale blue, light blue, and perhaps even something called "International Klein Blue."

And that last shade of blue underlines this whole discussion: your world expands when you go from not knowing what "International Klein Blue" looks like to identifying it when you see it. Yet in point of fact, your world expands and contracts because now you're likely to insist that such and such a shade is International Klein Blue, when prior to learning the label, you might have just said blue.

As we've seen (no pun intended), the label "blue" is at worst argumentative and at best imaginary. And if that's true of something as simple as the label for a color, what does that say about the rest of the labels in our lives?

Turning Blue with Cold

A monk asked his Zen master, "When cold or heat comes, how can we avoid it?"

The Zen master asked, "Why not go where there is no cold or heat?"

The monk said, "What do you mean by 'where there is no cold or heat'?"

The Zen master said, "When it's cold, cold kills you; when it's hot, heat kills you."

Zen Do

Zen tells us to *see—just so.*

The experience of seeing is yours and yours alone. You see from your perspective—and the bee sees from his/hers. Stopping to categorize/name/explain what you see is pointless and costs you here-and-now.

The world we see is so subtle, has so many items in it (that we as individuals, not necessarily as a species, don't know the names of), and has more shades of color and tint than could be enumerated in 10 lifetimes.

And you might want to tip your dry cleaner a few bucks for that lesson.

Famous Label, Brand-Name Zen

Ever wonder what the world was like before famous labels and brand names? Well, truer to what is *thus*, to be sure.

Yet these days it seems that everything "worth having"—and to an amazing degree, anyone "worth knowing" or "worth listening to"—is, to one degree or another, a famous label and/or a brand name. And please take particular note of the "and/or" in the previous sentence.

Oprah Winfrey is an example of someone who is a famous person, a famous label, and a famous brand. If the book, magazine, cause, movie, interview subject, or radio show content (to name just a few) is approved or endorsed by Oprah, a career can be made. And/or a fortune. Simply by Oprah (or Fill-In-The-Blank-With Your-Favorite-Celebrity) saying, in effect, "Yep."

On another tack, a medical doctor's endorsement of, say, anything, is another example. If the doctor says something is good (especially after all the training (s)he went through to become a doctor, we reason), whatever else the doctor might say about, well ... anything ... is probably also good.*

*This despite the fact that, as a good friend of mine once told me, "Somebody has to finish last in medical school."

Net result: we validate the celebrity/credentials of whomever said, "Yep", while simultaneously substituting in our mind their experience for ours. We're saying, in effect, "They are Big Names, so it must be good/so."

Then, as so often happens—your experience with whatever was the focus of their "Yep"—is different from theirs.

What do you feel? Do you feel disappointed, deceived, angry and/or even somewhat gullible? Does that in turn amplify the feeling(s) making them more pronounced, with the end result that you become a little more jaded about "the world."

Take heart. May I suggest a small libation?

Famous Self-Control

One day there was an earthquake that shook the entire Zen school. Parts of it even collapsed. Many of the students were terrified.

When the earthquake stopped, a teacher said, "Now you have had the opportunity to see how a Zen man behaves in a crisis situation.

You may have noticed that I did not panic. I was quite aware of what was happening and what to do. I led you all to the kitchen, the strongest part of the school. It was a good decision, because you see we have all survived without any injuries.

However, despite my self-control and composure, I did feel a little bit tense—which you may have deduced from the fact that I drank a large glass of milk, something I never do under ordinary circumstances."

One of the students smiled, but didn't say anything.

"What are you smiling at?" asked the teacher.

"That wasn't milk," the student replied, "it was a large glass of soy sauce."

Zen Do

There is no Zen but your Zen; no experience but your experience. With one exception (which you'll discover in just a moment), people who want to attach a Famous-Label or Brand Name to how you live, or what you think and say are trying to sell you something. Period, end of story.

Attaching their famous-maker brand names to your reality is bushwa. Bullshit. Crap. Drivel. Flim-flam. Hooey. Malarkey. Bunkum. Phooey. Guff. Hogwash. And 100% USDA Prime poppycock.

There is no Zen but your Zen. No experience but your experience. At best—at best—other people, whoever they are, act as fingers pointing at the moon—and that's it. You are your own famous-label, brand name Zen.

Can I have your autograph?

A Finely Written Painting in G Mixolydian

If I can beg your indulgence for just a couple of minutes, I'd like to create art.

Yes, you read me right. Here, on these very pages and before your very eyes, I will create (and perhaps destroy) art as most of you know it. (But before we get too far, you might want to make sure the kids are in another room.)

To begin, I'll need a perfectly ordinary blank piece of paper. Next, a typewriter into which I will insert the paper.

Now I'll need just a moment to compose myself before I create*.

(Pause)

OK. I'm ready to create now!

Turning my back so only I can see the paper.
Sounds of keystrokes.
Shoulders hunched in effort.

*We artists are always temperamental and sensitive to our environments, you know.

Emphatic breathing.
Now turning back to face you.

OK—I'm done. But before I show you my masterpiece, let me set the stage.

Like me, you may often find yourself surrounded by a sea of people talking about this or that piece of art (a movie, a painting, a dance, a theater production, a song, etc.) and speaking in rather authoritative tones about how the artist "missed the point" or "doesn't get it" or "has no idea what they're doing."

How many of us have listened to this or that person "educate" us on what constitutes "good fill-in the-blank art" (good music, good painting, good theater, good filmmaking, good acting, etc.)?

Yet one wonders how these folks even *perceived* the art before them, being wrapped in so many layers of belief. Yet the lesson had been taught to them from earliest childhood: beauty is in the eye of the beholder.

So is Zen.

Art and Incense

A long time ago in Japan, a woman made highly prized incense burners. She worked very slowly, taking a long time to craft each burner, and the result was always a masterpiece.

One day the mayor of this woman's city asked her to make him an incense burner. She accepted the commission and, as usual, took her time in creating her art for this most esteemed patron. Finally, after over half a year had passed, the new incense burner sat before her.

She spent much time studying the burner over the next days. She looked at it from every angle; she smoked, ate, drank, and meditated in front of it. Finally, she picked up a hammer and smashed the incense burner into a thousand tiny fragments.

It was not the perfect creation her mind demanded.

Zen Do

Art—which, to begin with and by definition, defies and eludes definition—is Zen, and is diminished by "explanation" and damaged by rationalization.* However, in everyday life, art has no need of words. Words—or the imperfect thoughts and images they convey—push the person experiencing the moment further away, be that a moment of art or a moment of Zen awakening.

How will knowing that one of the chords in *All Blues* by Miles Davis is a "G Minor 6 Add 9" bring you more enjoyment of the music? Moreover, in the time it takes to hear and think *about* this particular type of G chord, the music (and reality) have raced by. <u>Listen. Live the listening, don't think it away.</u>

How will thinking about the fact that Picasso usually painted women from life and not from memory enhance your enjoyment of *Sylvette*? Look. <u>Live the experience, don't think it away.</u>

To be sure, knowledge of the underlying forms and tools are important to the craftsperson, be (s)he a musician, a painter, or the maker of fine ceramics. Knowledge at this level makes it possible for the rest of us to experience great art.

*In academia, for educational purposes—that is a different animal and topic.

But each experience, like each work of art, is unique to the experiencer. *You* are the "expert" on the art you experience. The idea of a "common experience" of art is as flawed as the incense burner—and just as worthy of destruction by you.

Before I go, let me be clear: I'm not saying people should not study art/music/theater/etc. Having knowledge of these subjects is a fine thing—even a good career choice for some folks. There's little doubt that such knowledge may even increase your enjoyment and appreciation of the art in question.

My point here is an affirmation of the truism that "Beauty is in the eye of the beholder." Or the creator.

Oh—and my art?

It's in the palms of your hands.

Enjoy.

A Flour Sack of Zen

For some reason or other, there is a tendency for people to want things to be more complicated than they need to be, and clearly Zen has no time for this sort of "gilding the lily."

One of the odd things people have said to me about Zen is, "It seems like such a passive thing—all that sitting and meditating. I mean, what do you *do* in Zen?"

I usually smile, politely, at this because, as you may be discovering in reading this book, Zen is anything but passive—it is highly active, 100 percent immersive, and comprehensively participatory even to the smallest activity. Even an activity that might seem trivial.

But in Zen—nothing is trivial, and everything is a lesson.

A Flour Bag of Zen

A Zen adherent—often referred to in Zen literature as the Laughing Buddha and known for the linen sack he carried—was asked, "What is the significance of Zen?"

Without hesitation, our Zen friend silently placed his sack on the ground.

That was his answer.

The inquirer then asked, "So then, what is the actualization of Zen?"

Our friend instantly and silently picked up his sack, smiled, and walked away.

Zen Do

So:

Just here and now.

No preconceptions.

No dualistic thinking.

No religious abstractions.

No doctrine.

No symbols.

No beliefs.

No philosophy.

No noise, no theater, and no bullshit.

Just *thus*.

Mastering your mind takes effort. It is an active pursuit—whether your flour sack is up or down.

Where is yours?

How Do You Pronounce C. Everett Koop in Bahamian?

Walk along the right-hand side of Bay Street in Nassau, toward the bridge between New Providence and Paradise Island, and you'll come across a shoe store with several TVs set along the top of a row of display windows that front the sidewalk.

Last night and, for all I know, every night, the sidewalk in front of this store was illuminated by the glowing, televised image of the former surgeon general of the United States, the estimable Dr. C. Everett Koop. "Chick", to his friends.

Now, as peachy a guy as the eminent doctor was, seeing him droning on about things medical, at night, in the Bahamas, on TV screens, in a shoe store—decades after he left office as surgeon general in the Reagan administration—stopped my high-mileage tennies in their tracks and gave me pause to wonder: Someone thought putting Chick on an endless video loop in a shoe store window had value.

An interesting lesson that.

Tying Your Mind like a Cat

A Zen master ordered that the monastery's cat be tied up every evening when he and his students sat down for evening meditation, so as not to be bothered by the noise of the cat.

This practice went on for years. In fact, even after the original Zen master died, the cat continued to be tied up during the meditation session, and even when the original cat eventually died, yet another unfortunate cat was specifically brought to the monastery and tied up every night, just like the first. Then another cat and another and another through the centuries.

Across the years, students in the Zen monastery wrote many papers, books, and treatises—all explaining, with great reverence and symbolism, the need for, significance of, and meaning of tying up a cat before meditation practice.

Some still do.

Zen Do

I'm going to ask you some tough questions here:

- Ask yourself: How much of your life is ... ritual?
- Think: How much of what you do everyday is ... custom?
- Look Deeply: Is your marriage ... a habit?
- Reflect: Is your job/career ... rote?
- Ponder: Is your religion ... reflex?
- Consider: Is what you are doing with your life (as a whole)

what makes you ... happy? Or is what you think/believe is ... expected of you?

Here kitty-kitty*

*By the way, in Bahamian, it's pronounced C. Everett Koop.

I Haven't Seen Laurie in Fifteen Years

Laurie and I are close personal friends. That notwithstanding, until recently, I hadn't actually seen Laurie in fifteen years. A while back, we met again in San Francisco after all these years. I won't kid you, it was great seeing her, and I flatter myself to think she felt the same way. It was a bit awkward, but what meeting of old friends who haven't seen each other in a long time isn't?

If you'd been there, watching from a discrete distance, of course, you would have seen two people greet each other warmly, exchange hugs, and you'd even get to see a nice example of a Well Executed Friend Kiss (… or two.) OK, *three*.

But you wouldn't have seen Kris.

And you wouldn't have seen Laurie.

You see, we weren't there.

I'll explain in a moment.

Knowing Life in an Apple

Glen, who taught Zen in St. Louis, Missouri brought his class together by placing an apple on the table beside him and saying, "We are going to have a little contest tonight. See this apple? Whoever can explain apples best will win and go on a retreat to the Zen Center of San Francisco with me next weekend."

Susan raised her hand and began explaining the origin of the apple as a fruit and its introduction to the United States. She even mentioned Johnny Appleseed.

Bill raised his hand and went into considerable detail about the various forms of apples such as applesauce, cider, desserts, and so on.

A third student, Barbara, said nothing. She reached into her backpack and extracted a small folding Swiss Army knife attached to her key chain. With it, she cut a wedge from the apple, slipped it into Glen's mouth, and used her hands to gently move his jaws up-and-down so the apple would squish inside his mouth.

Glen smiled after swallowing the apple and said, "Exactly so. Apples cannot be explained with words. Apples must be experienced on the tongue and in the mouth. The only way to know apples is with your mouth shut."

Zen Do

You change. I changed. Laurie changed. We all change.

Change is what life is.

The Laurie I thought I knew ("Old Laurie") is a figment of my imagination. Selected memories highly polished and very highly curated. Reflections, thoughts, dreams, words handpicked by my ego to make me feel good about her—and about myself.

That's what we do, we selectively curate ideas, impressions, and needs about who or what someone is/was/should be. And whatever those curated ideas are, they are not one thing: the Laurie I knew back-in-the-day. Old Laurie is the very embodiment of a lie, of missing out on life, on today, on *thus*.

There is/was/will always be only one way to "know" Laurie and to "see" Laurie again—by experiencing her in the *then-and-there*, in the *here-and-now*.

And doing so mindfully, with my eyes wide open, and judging, opinionated, comparison-oriented monkey mind silenced, and mouth shut.

Except for, you know, the kiss. Or two. *Three...*

If'ing Your Life Away

I wonder how many people you know personally to whom the following description applies:

- Start many a conversation with, "I've finally figured it out. Now if I can only ..."
- Or, seem be constantly starting long explanations with "If only ..." or "When I ..."

Sound familiar? Thought so.

If, no pun intended, a key difference between an adept in Zen and one who is not is that the adept understands that apart from Buddha nature there is no nature, you can say, "If only ..." all you wish, but wishing or wanting or what-if'ing builds mental constructs that isolate you from your original Buddha nature. Another difference is that the adept in Zen has realized that in truth, in reality, there are no ifs, only *is*.

For example, the sun doesn't shine *if* ... The sun shines.

A bird doesn't fly *if* ... it flies.

Your liver doesn't filter blood *if* ... it filters.

When I drop a ten-pound weight, it doesn't fall *if* ... it falls.

A person doesn't have Buddha nature if (s)he has studied the sutras and zazen. A person *is* Buddha nature.

"If" is often a code word for "In order to escape reality, or so as to not face reality, I'm going to construct a new view of life, or a new idea of life, or a new paradigm for life, or well, **anything** other than be here now in this moment and simply do the next thing to be done."

And the trouble with all this if'ing is twofold: first, because the if'ing is *about* something/someone/some experience and is not direct experience.

Secondly, the if'ing creates another layer of abstraction or delusion between truth and the person doing the if'ing. And that's just plain if'ed up.

If You Wobble

If'ing comes in many flavors besides plain old vanilla "if." It often disguises itself as "when."

There is a well-known saying in Zen that goes something like this:

"In sitting, just sit.

In standing, just stand.

Above all—don't wobble."

Zen Do

Zen teaches us to not if, and to not when—and above all, to not wobble. And wobble, is also a code word for if'ing.

Examine your life. Do you see yourself if'ing? For example, do you find yourself saying things like:

- *If only my husband would ...*
- *If my wife would just stop ...*
- *If my ship comes in ...*
- *If only I had that (job, house, car, money, date, etc.) ...*
- *If people would just ...*
- *If I could just find the time to ...*
- *If these troubles of mine would just ...*
- *If there was just ...*
- *If I master Zen ...*
- *"If I were a rich man* ..."*

Examine what it is that drives *you* to "if." Life is in the doing and the living, in the here and now, and in this moment—there is no "if" in reality. (BTW..."when" is often a code word for "if.")

"If" is a convenient escape-the-moment drug, an appealing mental salve for a wounded ego, a favorite club for bashing other people's egos as a way of soothing yours, and a big ripcord handle that's so **easy** to pull when you want to parachute out of a mental trap (of your own making, naturally.) Or, on too many occasions for some, to get out of responsibility.

"If" is also like yesterday/tomorrow, leprechauns, wishful thinking, and up-without-down—phantoms, imaginary con-

*Sorry. I couldn't resist.

structs, mirages, delusions, hallucinations, phantasms, optical illusions, chimera, a head trip, a misimpression, and a will-o-the-wisp.

The Zen path is to go straight.

IF—you want things to happen in life, you have to get up and make them happen. Period. Opportunity and if'ing aren't going to come skipping hand-in-hand to knock on your front door.

So take a look at your path, your life, and see if you are going straight—or are you if'ing your life away.

Instant Zen Just Ain't Fast Enough

There was a fascinating story on Yahoo News awhile back. It seems Americans like things fast. How fast? I'll let the story speak for itself …

> "WASHINGTON—*By Calvin Woodward, Associated Press Writer—We'll make this quick. We know you're busy. An Associated Press poll has found an impatient nation. To get to the point without further ado, it's a nation that gets antsy after five minutes on hold on the phone and 15 minutes max in a line. So say people in the survey.*
>
> *The Department of Motor Vehicles, the U.S. version of the old Soviet bread line, is among the top spots where Americans hate to wait. But grocery stores are the worst. Almost one in four in the poll picked the grocery checkout as the line where their patience is most likely to melt like the ice cream turning to goo in their cart.*
>
> *And it seems people don't mellow with age. The survey found older people to be more impatient than younger people. Nor does getting away from the urban pressure cooker make much difference.*

People in the country and the suburbs can bear a few more minutes in a line before losing it than city inhabitants can, but that's it.

In short, Americans want it all NOW. Or awfully close to now."

That is true of Zen as well. In explaining Zen, I've noticed a tendency for the listener to want a short, encapsulated, concise, easy-to-understand-without-too-much-thought description/explanation.

The short version, in other words. That's where the rub is.

See, as a general rule of thumb, I'm all in favor of being as productive as possible, so time spent laboring over an explanation about, say, Zen wouldn't rate high on my to-do list, either. On the other hand, as a ground rule, when we learn something, it usually takes time, often more time than we anticipate, to really get to "know" something.

Yet both of those statements have problems from the get-go.

To begin with, I have no interest in learning *about* something. If I'm going to take the time to learn it, I want to *learn it*, not learn *about* it. One is, for example, reading *about* skydiving, and the other is leaping headfirst out of a perfectly good airplane.

Staying in that vein, you wouldn't want to read the *Cliff Notes* version of *How to Skydive* and then try a high altitude low opening (HALO) jump (read: a very dangerous form of skydiving) from, say, 23,000 feet, would you?

Well—not without a good bowl of soup.

Soup's Secret Ingredient

A Zen master, known far and wide as an excellent if simple cook, invited a famous, and notoriously impatient, samurai to dinner at the master's house. Greeting the samurai warmly, the master led him into the dining room, excused himself, and went into the kitchen.

Not a small amount of time passed. The samurai called after the master, asking if perhaps the master had forgotten him. The master reappeared.

"I apologize for the delay, but dinner is coming along well now. It shouldn't be long." And with that, the master returned to the kitchen.

More time passed, and the samurai's patience began to chafe. Again he called for the Zen master, who once again entered the dining room.

"Please forgive me. This is taking longer than I anticipated, but I assure you it is worth the wait."

And with that, the Zen master once again returned to the kitchen.

Finally, after an even longer interval, the master entered the dining room with a steaming bowl of miso soup. The samurai began to eat, lavishing great praise on the soup. The master deferred such praise, insisting, "It's just miso soup."

When the samurai finished the bowl of soup, he once again showered the master in praise for this savory dish, begging him to reveal the secret to such a praiseworthy dish.

The master sat quietly for a moment and then said, "Well, it does have one special ingredient, I will admit." The samurai begged to understand what this was.

The master replied: "It took time."

Zen Do

Everything should take as long as it takes to learn and no longer, so don't be in a rush, but neither tarry.

Seeing Zen can take a lifetime—or a microsecond. Or lots of individual microseconds. In either case, thousands of years of teaching, thousands of books and speeches on the subject, combined with thousands of anecdotes and the personal experience of billions of practitioners say the same thing: it will simply take as long as it takes—so be mindful and stop worrying about it.

Soup's on!

Your Path: On a Sine Wave

Mornings: meditation, tea, my cats, and the morning paper. Oh, and the obituaries, of course—gotta have the obits!

No, I'm not some sort of ghoul who finds fiendish pleasure in reading about people shuffling off this mortal coil*; or any such nonsense. Actually, my interest in the obituaries is quite the opposite—it's a celebration of life, an affirmation of the sine wave of Zen.

I'll explain.

Remember sine waves from high school math class? They look something like this:

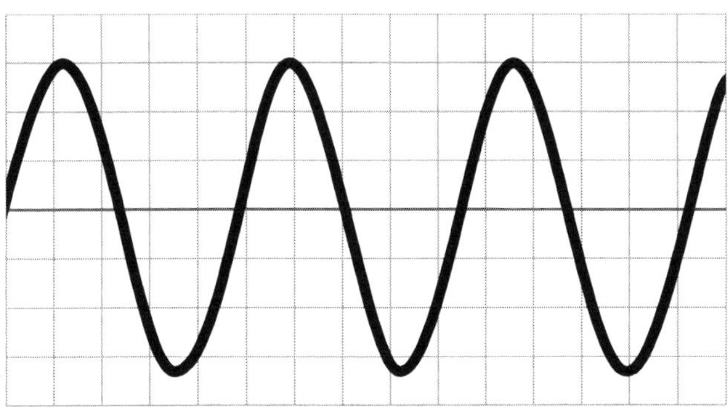

*... Zombie conga line, pushing up daises, etc, etc, etc.

Then you probably also remember that a sine wave is actually a representation of 360 degrees of a circle. The upslope of the wave starts at "zero" (a flat line that bisects the entire sine wave), then rises to 90 degrees, then falls 90 degrees, returning to zero and completing a 180-degree (or half-circle) trip. This trip up to 90 degrees and back down to zero is the "positive" portion of the sine wave. And as we all also remember, basic math postulates that for every positive number, there is a negative number. For every up, there is a down.*

So next, the wave plunges under the flat line to minus 90 degrees, then rises again 90 degrees back to zero, completing another 180-degree trip. This voyage under the flat line is referred to as the negative portion of the sine wave. Add the two 180-degree trips together and you get a circle—and a wave. You also get ...

Positive and negative.
Wave and trough.
Above and below.

And lots of other opposites.

Living and dying.
Coming and going.
On and off.

Dualistic, to be sure, but very useful to this discussion. And arbitrary.

Where does a circle start? Where does a circle end? Sure, we have the whole so-many-degrees thing—but that's just as arbitrary. Who decided that a degree was as wide as we determine a degree to be?

There is no start and no end to the rebirth of a sine wave, or a circle, or *reality*—or us.

* To everything (turn, turn, turn) / There is a season (turn, turn, turn) / And a time to every purpose, under heaven—The Byrds, 1965. Classic.

Yep—we can learn much Zen from the humble sine wave.

Coming, Going, Gone

Just before a man died, a Zen master came to visit.

The master asked, "Shall I lead you on?"

The man said, "I came here alone, I shall go alone."

The master said, "If you think you really come and go, that is your delusion. Let me show you the path on which there is no coming and no going."

The man understood the master's words, smiled—and passed away.

Zen Do

I'll make you a deal—go read the obituaries. Like a sine wave which never starts nor stops, which has no beginning and no ending, the obits are themselves an indicator of the path on which there is no coming and no going.

The obits are also a celebration of *life*. The stories the obits tell of full lives, quiet lives, huge adventurous lives, delicate quiet lives—are all celebrations of *life*.

Life is a 360 degree, full sine wave event. It doesn't matter if you are at degree 1 or degree 359, *here and now IS life. Live yours and celebrate it every minute of every day!*

Because the wave will always be. And you are the wave.

Murder on the Zen Express

With apologies to Agatha Christie, how's this for a scene from a movie:

THE SCENE: Inside a dank police interrogation room. One naked light bulb sways from the ceiling.

THE PLAYERS: One Zen student (that would be me). Two sweaty, mean, ham-fisted, hard-boiled homicide detectives.

ACTION!

First Detective: "You might as well spill it. We've got you red-handed. You left a trail of evidence a blind man could follow, fella."

Second Detective: "Yeah ... come on ... you'll feel better if you tell us. Go ahead—make our day."

Me: "OK, OK, stop! I, I ... I confess, I confess, I did it! Every single day ... every ... single ... day ... I tried to kill someone. And sometimes .... I've succeeded. That's right: one by one, I tried to cut up my counselors, murder my masters, terminate my teachers, lynch my leaders—and even bludgeon the Buddha to death. And there's more ...... you'd probably find out anyway, so I might as well tell you … I have an accomplice! It is my … Zen master! He told me to kill them!"

(Insert spooky music here … and fade to black.)

OK—so I don't have to worry about a career as a mystery writer. But there is more than a germ of truth in my salty scene writing—it is true that every day I try to kill someone or something. Every *single* day. And sometimes, I am successful—and my Zen master really did tell me to do it (*Evil laugh…*).

The Case of the Dead Buddha

A famous Zen koan (and my Zen master) says: "If you meet the Buddha, kill him."

Snuff said.

Zen Do

Do you want to find Buddha? I have a clue for you then, Chief Inspector:

Clue #1: Stop looking outside yourself for Buddha. Looking "outside" has two problems. First, in Buddhism the dualism of inside/outside—just ain't so.

Second, the Buddha you look for out (t)here—just ain't there. Put another way: seeking Buddha/your Buddha nature outside yourself is like looking for your hat while wearing your hat.

Sure, there are lots of "fingers pointing at the moon" in the shape of books, videos, teachers, schools, etc which teach "about" a/the Buddha, blah, blah, blah.*

*And yes, I get that this book is both a pointing finger AND a blah, blah, blah…

But in your mind, the Buddha, other teachers, even the author of this fine, quality book you're reading now (ahem...) are merely mental experiences which distract you from reality. You don't want such a distraction from your path of awakening/enlightenment. (Aside from, you know, this fine quality book you're reading now...)

So, when in your mind you find the Buddha or one of those other fingers pointing at the moon—well, it's like Humphrey Bogart might say, "Look here, Kid. It's either you or them. What'ya waiting for. Forget Paris. Now let 'em have it!"

(Insert spooky music here and fade to black.)

Parking Lot Zen

Recently I was in the parking lot of a grocery store. I thought I was driving correctly, but apparently, unknown to me, I had strayed a few inches across the painted line that separates incoming from outgoing traffic.

At that moment, a truck with two folks inside came toward me in the incoming traffic lane—and came to an abrupt halt parallel to my car. The driver of the truck rolled down his window and began reading an unfiltered and unadulterated version of the "Riot Act" because, among the rest, I'd committed the "crime" of crossing said dividing line.

I would have apologized (if I'd had the opportunity), but the other driver was having much too good a time describing me in terms so colorful and profane, I'm convinced three *real* truck drivers got out of the business just hearing the nonstop torrent of obscenities being sent my way.

Notwithstanding, I did voice an apology as I drove away.

About fifteen minutes later, and now relocated to the natural foods aisle of the grocery store, I heard a voice in an adjacent aisle speaking into what must have been a cell phone about a "ridiculous, idiotic driver who crossed a line in the parking lot and caused me to slam on my brakes" and how this "moron" had "just ruined my day and ruined my week."

Naturally, I couldn't resist a peek around the end of the grocery isle. Yep—it was the driver I'd "offended" earlier.

I hastened to complete my shopping and get outta Dodge. After all, there were other lines in this parking lot and, well, you know how I drive ...

Is That So?

A Zen master was confronted by a beautiful girl and her family. It seems the girl was recently delivered of a baby girl and had accused the master of being the child's father. The master's response was, "Is that so?"

The master took the child in, worked hard, and cared for her in all particulars for the next year. After that time, the child's mother and her parents returned to the master and told him the mother had lied and that the master was not the father of the child.

The master's response as he returned the child was, "Is that so?"

Zen Do

How often we leave reality and replace it with, of all things, imaginary imagery such as the image of a reckless and godless driver bent on tearing down civilization as we know it and sending us all into the bottomless pit of eternal damnation—by crossing, by a few inches, a painted line in a parking lot.

Yet because we build images, bad guys, villains, enemies, friends, models, constructs, stories, excuses, and other delusions in our minds, we regularly abandon the real living of our lives. On both sides of the traffic line, we invent abuses, insults, and entire sagas worthy of a TV miniseries about—absolutely nothing of real importance.

So the next time you find yourself projecting mental models (or a stream of venom) at someone instead of living in the moment (or just living-and-let-live) ask yourself, "Is that so?"

Then remember the lessons the Zen master in our story taught us about character, judgment, equanimity, language, patience, and acceptance.

They are so.

Pissed-Off Zen

Among the many aspects in which Zen has had a profound impact on my life is this: my temper.

Back in the day, as they say, I used to keep a crate of cheap clock radios in my bedroom. And every few months I'd have to order a new crate.

Were the clocks defective? Not in the slightest. The person who bought the alarm clocks was defective.

Here's how it worked: I would wake up to the alarm so mad at its temerity of waking me that I would physically grab the offending clock and throw it across the room, smashing it to pieces.

Then I'd get out of bed, clean up the mess of broken clock radio parts, reach into the crate, open a box, and plug in a new clock radio. I felt bad in a way about the clocks, but I was convinced that I just had a "bad temper," and some days circumstances and events just "made it worse."

Thank goodness, those days are long past and I've had the same clock radio for years.

And what occasioned this change in my attitude? Was it therapy, or perhaps a new antidepressant drug? Was it being "born again," which I haven't? Was it possibly the need for rotator cuff surgery in my clock-pitching shoulder? (Which, oddly enough, I did have done.)

The answer, which I of course previewed earlier in this story, is "none of the above." For me, Zen brought me face-to-face with the root cause and source of my temper: my monkey mind.

Show Me, Zen

A Zen student went to his master and said, "Master, I have a terrible temper. How can I cure it?"

The master said, "You have something very odd. Please let me see what you have."

The student replied, "Well, I can't show it to you just now."

And the master asked, "Well, when *can* you show it to me?"

The student said, "I don't know—it arises unexpectedly."

"In that case," the master said, "it is not of your true nature. If it were, you could show it to me anytime. When you were born it was not there, and your parents didn't give it to you. Perhaps you should think this over."

The Zen student, enlightened, bowed.

Zen Do

Begin by taking inventory. Meditate on this topic for yourself. Perhaps you too lay claim to something (such as a bad temper, a lazy work ethic, a habit of postponing things, or an ungovernable appetite), which, as we've just seen, is clearly *not* part of your true nature, yet for/of which you've said was not your fault, or was out of your control, or requires professional help.

Perhaps upon reflection, you too will see that an ungovernable temper, for example, isn't something to be medicated, or confined, or even treated, by anyone but you.

In some cases it may well be, but perhaps not in your case. Zen teaches us that you are not your thoughts of yourself—good or bad. You are not the labels, good or bad, that you or someone else has stuck on you. Nor are you the idea, good or bad, of yourself, or anyone else's idea of who or what you should/could/would be.

You *are* Buddha. All that you are and need you already have. Except perhaps for some advice on how to locate/relocate what it is you are/have.

So who, or what, is stopping you now? "Throw" it/or them away and never "buy" another.

Then rollover and grab another 10 winks.

Real Zen Is Not Lacking

People always want to know what "real Zen" is like. They'll say, "I see the word 'Zen' all over the place, but what is Zen *really* like? I want to learn that—I want to learn *real Zen*."

Like countless Zen students and "moon-finger-pointers" down through the ages, my answers are often not exactly what the person doing the questioning expects.

"Real Zen is the grass bending."

"Real Zen is who you are between your thoughts."

"Real Zen is, what was your great-grandfather's shoe size?"

"Real Zen is what makes you put out a retraining arm to protect your child even before you hit the brakes in your car to avoid an accident you didn't see coming one-tenth of a second ago."

"Real Zen is remembering a forgotten name."

"Real Zen is why you cry every time it starts to snow."

"Real Zen is living life without the fatal hesitancy of thought."

"Real Zen, is Moonbeam Shoo-fly Guacamole."

en Story

Lin-Chi said, "I tell you, there's no Buddha, no Dharma, no practice, no enlightenment. Yet you go off trying to find ... *something*. Blind fools! Will you put another head on the one you have? *What is it that you lack?*"

Zen Do

You want more?

Like the man said: "*What is it that you lack?*"

We're done here.

The Satori of Fender Benders

In an average year, 18,000 or so traffic accidents per day occur in the United States. With an average of 2 cars per accident, 36,000 people, give or take, per day are in those accidents.

Add to that the number of people who drive by—at .0003 miles per hour, rubbernecking at the scene—and you conservatively get another 20 people per accident and a new total of 396,000 people. But we're not done yet.

Add in at least two officials (ambulance, police, fire department, etc.) on average per accident, and you add in another 36,000 people, giving us a total of over 425,000 people in, looking at, or responding to accidents every day.

That's a flock of folks. A peck of people. Mucho mouth-breathers. And oodles of onlookers.

I mention all of this sketchy statistical score-keeping because I drove to the grocery store about an hour ago and witnessed just one of today's allotment of accidents. Sure enough, police and an ambulance were on the scene, rubberneckers were in full boom, and I was reminded of how useful a scene like that can be for reminding one of the need for continued (actually, continuous) Zen practice.

Actually, continuous is the key: the next time you witness or happen upon a basic fender bender, notice how you feel—notice the change in your perception of you and the world around you. Perhaps it's something like this:

- You think, "Better you than me, Buddy." Followed quickly by "Poor guy."
- You do an astonishingly rapid check of "Am I OK?"—even if you were blocks away when the accident happened.
- You are suddenly a candidate for the Safest Driver on the Road award.
- You look at, then chide yourself for looking at, the accident while reminding yourself that two seconds ago you were silently cursing the drivers in front of you, wondering why they couldn't just "drive on—there's nothing to look at."
- You are aware, quite distinctly, of the feel of the steering wheel, of the gas and brake pedals, of the weight and ride of your car on the road, and of the feel of the road itself.

In general, awareness becomes very real, very focused.

Living, Not Focusing

A Zen master was approached by a twelve-year-old boy who sought instruction in Zen.

The master said, "You are too young," but, in short, the child insisted, so the master finally agreed.

The master said to the boy, "You can hear the sound of two hands when they clap together. Show me the sound of one hand."

The young man bowed and went away to consider this problem. From the window of his room, he could hear music. "Ah, I have it!" he proclaimed.

The next evening, when the Zen master asked him to illustrate the sound of one hand, the boy began to play music.

"No," the Master said, "that will never do. That is not the sound of one hand. Try again."

Time and again the boy appeared before the master: "The sound of one hand is ..."

- Dripping water
- The cry of an owl
- The sound of the wind
- The sounds of locusts
- The sound of Frank Zappa's "*Watch Out Where the Huskies Go, Don't You Eat That Yellow Snow*", played backwards on a vintage turntable.

All of his answers were rejected by the master.

For almost a year, the boy pondered what the sound of one hand might be.

Finally, he entered true meditation and transcended all sounds. "I could collect no more," he explained later, "so I reached the soundless sound."

He had realized the sound of one hand.

Zen Do

A few other things seem to happen when you observe an accident as well:

- No matter what (family or money problems, health concerns, relationship issues—whatever) you were thinking of disappeared from your mind in a microsecond.
- The air seems to taste better, colors seem more defined, you see people, cars, and other things with crystal clarity and focus, and your senses in general are heightened.
- Here and now seem real important.
- You feel connected in some vague, hard-to-describe way with what you're seeing.

In short, you snap out of thinking *about* and snap-back to *reality*.

Reality and Zen are living. The rest is Monkey Mind Window Dressing.

In the same way that "water dripping" is not the sound of one hand clapping, and an accident is not something that should bring you back to reality.

Life and reality move at a billion-trillion-trillion (B-T-T) light-years per second*, and being in the moment requires your active participation and attention for every one of those B-T-T seconds.

*It's the most ridiculously fast number I could think of.

If you're thinking *about* something instead of mindfully living **each** moment, not only will you not know the sound of one hand, but as sure as higher post-accident insurance premiums, you're headed straight for another unpleasant sight: that of the wreckage of a life spent not living in, *reality*.

Scrooge Zen

I'm curious—by a show of hands, how many of you have read or seen Charles Dickens's *A Christmas Carol*? Many; that's very good—and as expected. After all, in one form or another, it's been a holiday staple for generations.

But I wonder—have you ever reflected less on the stinginess of Scrooge and more on the Zen of Scrooge? You weren't aware of the Zen in this Dickensian classic? There is, as Marley's ghost says, "Much."

In fact, one particular Zen lesson concerns Marley's ghost and the chain he wears, which, he informs Scrooge, he (Marley) made "link by link and yard by yard." He goes on to warn Scrooge that his (Scrooge's) own chain was "as full, and as long, as this seven years ago, and you have labored on it since, it is a *ponderous* chain!"

Yet Scrooge is unaware of this fetter. He sees no chains. He doesn't feel heavy. He recalls no specific "labor" on these or any other chains—much like many of us.

In our daily lives, many of us too do not see or feel "the weight and length of the strong coil" we bear. Moreover, for many of us, it isn't that we've labored on our chains these past seven years as Scrooge has—we've labored on our chains since we were children. Right about the point where we starting figuring that we knew who was right and who was wrong and what was good and what was bad.

The Light of Zen

A student approached a Zen master to ask if he could study with him. The master said, "Perhaps, but first you have to pass a very difficult and demanding test—but if you're willing to at least try, and perhaps succeed, then I would be willing to take you as a student."

The student agreed.

The master took the student to an imposing looking door and said, "In this room there are hundreds of black, razor-tipped bamboo stakes, in the walls, in the floor, and hanging from the ceiling. The stakes are coated in the fastest acting poison on Earth. Even the slightest, briefest touch of one stake conveys enough poison to kill 10 men instantly—and you can't see these stakes for the room is dark as a tomb. If you can safely cross the room and exit into the hallway beyond, I will take you as my student."

The student nodded his agreement to the task, was blindfolded, and was guided into the room. The door clanged behind him. He removed the blindfold and, indeed, the room was pitch black.

After several hours the student, worn and covered in sweat from his exertion, emerged from the exit door. He blinked in the hallway light and smiled triumphantly at the master.

The teacher promptly accepted him as a student and said, "And now you are ready for your first lesson."

He opened the door to the room and turned on a light, flooding the room with brightness. The room was absolutely bare and empty from wall to wall and floor to ceiling.

The Zen master said, "Your progress from the entry door to this door—this is how you have lived your life until now. It is clearly time to change."

Zen Do

We routinely see what we want to see not what *reality* gives us to *see*.

We move carefully and painstakingly around objects in the dark (beliefs in our mind as to how and what things are) that aren't even there.

We burden and bury ourselves under the weight and length of ideas, concepts, fixations, and "knowledge" every bit as invisible as Scrooge's chains and every bit as nonexistent as the razor-tipped bamboo stakes.

But the good news is that, as was true for Scrooge, succor is at hand.

To be *mindful*, to be fully *awake*, like Scrooge when he experiences his reclamation, is to be "as light as a feather."

See your chains—and use your Zen practice to not only smash them, but to protect yourself from ever forging even one more link. *Seeing reality* gives you the sight to sprint across any darkened room in your mind.

Welcome to Zen, Scrooge.

The Secret Code Word of Zen

Ever found yourself in this situation? You go to, say, the Grand Canyon, and when you peer down into its awesome majesty and grandeur, the one and only word that springs to your lips, completely unbidden, is: "Wow.*"

Psssst! Don't look now, but you've discovered the Secret Code Word of Zen.

As we've discussed, much of Zen training concerns getting students to here, to now, to this moment. To reality, if you will. (True, they start out as concepts to new Zen students, but the objective of the exercise is still valid.)

Zen teachers will sometimes shout, surprise, or even whack a student with a stick to snap said student into the moment. Zen anecdotes tell of students who found satori (awakening) as a result.

Alternatively, some Zen teachers will use the repetition of a word or sound—"Mu" (No) and "Om" are common examples—to stop the mind from its wanderings and focus it here and now.

*Yeah, I can hear your parents now, "Wow? All that college education shot to hell..."

And some Zen teachers will use quite ordinary stories or situations to help illuminate or illustrate Zen, based on the idea that confronting reality in everyday life will, and does, help snap students into awakening.

Now—if as a result of one (some, or even all) of these methods or others, you saw, with crystal clarity, that the moment in which you're reading this is all of eternity, and what you see around you is all of reality, wouldn't *your* next thought be ... "Wow!"?

Wow is a good analogy for the mind that doesn't cling to concepts. Wow is beyond definition—you can indicate what you said wow to, but no one can explain what wow *is*.

The Hair's Breadth Canyon

A monk asked a Zen master, "A hair's breadth of difference—and what happens?"

The master replied, "Heaven and earth are far away."

The monk continued, "And when there is not a hair's breadth of difference?"

The master replied, "Heaven and earth are far away."

Zen Do

The Zen master is making a couple of key points here:

1: You cannot be almost enlightened on a given point. Enlightenment either is or isn't. It's binary: 1/0, on/off, is/isn't. (And no this has nothing to do with dualism.) If you are a hair's breadth from enlightenment you are 100 miles away.

2: The questions being asked, in this case, have no meaning. They are irrelevant, they are things which cannot be asked and answered, they can only be experienced. If you have enlightenment on that point, you *see*. If not, it is hot air, and a waste of everyone's time.

On the one hand, "Wow" is what most people say when words fail them. There is typically no concrete thought coterminous with someone saying "Wow." Most often there are just free floating words (if that) scattered across a mind rent blank by the image being presented to it.

The mind that is stunned into not being able to talk, that cannot "find the words" (beyond "Wow") is still the mind that can beat your heart and cause you to breathe.

Go there!

"Oh, wow."

The Story of Life in a Broken Cup

When dealing with children, and also with people whom we feel are not quite as "with it" as we might like to think we are, there is a tendency to tell the person in question "How Things Are" with a finality which brooks little argument, no matter how politely murmured and delicately veiled the "How Things Are" was rendered.

And **nowhere** are dictums on "How Things Are" delivered with more authority than on the subject of the end of life.

Pick your vantage point—Egyptian mummification, Tree Burial, Cryogenics, Funerary Cannibalism, Resomation, Plastination, turning Aunt Betty's ashes into a Memorial Diamond*, turning Uncle Bob's ashes into part of a concrete "Memory Reef" off a convenient coastline, sending Dear Cousin Murgatroyd to her reward by way of "bio-cremation" in which a chemical solution is used to dissolve bodily tissue into a clear, sterile liquid that can be safely poured down a handy nearby drain, or spending $150 to put some ashes of the dear departed into a hand-blown glass pendant that you can "wear as a necklace or

*Seriously, memorial diamonds are a real thing. You could look it up.

hang from your rear-view mirror," the company says—death is **the** area where "Because I said so", "That's just the way it is!", "Everyone knows!", or "Because (insert deity name here) said so" reigns supreme.

Yet when many of us are actually confronted with death, these models shatter in an instant—splintered by the force of the way things *really* are.

Enlightenment Is Child's Play

A young student studied with a Zen teacher who owned a precious, one-of-a-kind collectible antique teacup. One day the boy accidentally broke the cup. Looking at what had happened, the boy attained insight.

Hearing his master's footsteps, he hid the fragments of the broken teacup behind his back and asked his teacher, "Master, why do people have to die?"

"This is natural," explained the master, "everything has to die and has just so long to live."

The boy produced the fragments of the broken relic and said, "It was time for your cup to die."

Zen Do

Look around your life—in your house, at your car, in your office—where are your "rare teacups"? Is your "teacup" a vintage Mercedes? Or a violin handed down from father to son over many generations? Perhaps yours is a ring or a watch that cost a small fortune. Or equally precious beliefs, views, or opinions.

And perhaps the teacup you hold dearest is ... your life.

Whatever your particular "teacup", take a moment and look at it closely. Now—imagine that the "teacup" is gone, shattered into the fragments that the boy swept behind his back. See him present them to you and tell you it was time for your "teacup" to die.

Eventually, everything becomes a broken teacup. Everything came from the one source and returns ultimately to that source—you, me, gold, empires, religions, Hallmark greeting cards, Grandma, your best work, your worst excuse, Ronald McDonald, galaxies, Hugh Hefner*, and, yes, teacups.

Meditate on the truth that everything composite returns to the source, and on this question—when the teacup is your life, or the life of your wife, husband, maybe even your child, what will you say to the boy/doctor/pastor/whomever, when (s)he tells you it was/is time for that particular teacup to die?

*It was a chore getting Mr. Playboy into this book, but if you'll overlook the pictures, (yeah, yeah, I know...) in its heyday *Playboy* magazine contained some of the best examples of interviews, non-fiction articles and short story writing in American journalism. Very nice work, Hugh.

Secret Zen

I have a secret, a private little secret I've never told anyone before. It's embarrassing, really—a deep character flaw that might get more than its share of frowns if the word ever got out.

Ok—I'll let the word out!

My secret is .... I smile at Zen newbies. There—I've said it.

Now, to be fair, I never let on about my smile, you understand, and I'm almost always careful to conceal or mask my smile—but on the right occasion it's there nonetheless: a genuine, 100% 'Born in the USA'*, corners-raised, toothpaste-ad-ready, Chiclet-toothed, mouth twister of a smile. And what triggers this display of my pearly whites? It isn't that here is a new student to Zen—I'm not cruel or some sort of sick-o. No, far from it.

Rather, I smile every time I hear a Zen teacher look a newbie in the eye and say, "I don't have anything to teach you."

Why do I smile at this seemingly innocuous (and, to some, perplexing) utterance?

* Your welcome, Bruce!

Because few folks new to Zen realize they just received one of the best lessons and/or koans there are in Zen.

We're taught from youngest childhood that acquisition of "knowledge" is the road to wealth, power, riches, and happiness. From the derisive attack of "You don't know anything!" to the double-bind circular logic of "I can't hire you—you don't have enough experience for this job." "But how can I get the experience you want if you don't hire me for the job?" to bumper-sticker philosophies like "He who dies with the most toys wins," to admonitions from dime-store Zen master wannabes that "I alone can show you the way!,*" we're taught that the road to all is paved with accumulation.

Well—as one of the greatest Zen masters of contemporary years famously and frequently said, "Not necessarily so."

A Degree in Nothing

A Zen master said, "What is the purpose of pilgrimage?"

His student replied, "I don't know."

The master said, "Not knowing is most intimate."

Zen Do

The path of Zen means being open to the way things actually are. Period. No religion, words, or magic pixie dust.

We don't try to run and hide behind our beliefs, and we don't try to force the universe of reality to conform to our views, our

*Call for Donald J. Trump!

delusions, or our prejudices and preferences. We're open to what is: joy, pain, suffering, relief, happiness, or anything else.

Not knowing, not clinging, trusting openness without defense or excuses... this is joining with Buddha in the absolute.

Therefore, there is nothing to "teach."

So—the next time you see me, take a peek and see if I'm smiling.

It may be because I've just heard a Zen teacher (perhaps *you*) tell yet another newbie that (s)he has nothing to teach.

Or—it could be because I've just whispered to myself, "This humble writer has nothing to teach you, either."

Shhhhh ... it's a secret.

Seven Years to a New Bob

Want to increase the inventory of strange looks you've received in your life? Ask people to point to themselves, specifically.

Or better yet, let's take Bob—a purely fictional person I just whipped up for use in this chapter. (He won't mind being asked ...)

To all outward appearances, Bob is a normal-looking guy: 37 years old, 6 feet 2 inches tall, 210 pounds, neatly trimmed brown hair, hazel eyes, athletic walk. Married, Bob has 2 kids, a family dog, a good job, and a nice middle-class home*.

You know this guy.

He's just like thousands of other "Bobs" you've met in your life. In fact, Bob may live right next door to you.

Now—imagine walking up to Bob and saying this: "Bob, point to Bob. Point to 'you,' Bob." Naturally, Bob is going to look at you a bit quizzically, give you some sort of cautious smile, and point to himself.

Then say this: "No, that's not quite what I'm looking for, Bob. That's your body. Where is 'Bob'?"

*He also bites his nails. Pass it on...

Again, Bob will look at you curiously, point to himself again (perhaps a bit more slowly), and say to you (even more slowly, as if you have some sort of learning defect), and say, "I. Am. Bob."

Say this: "No, Bob. 'Bob' is a sound, a noise, a vocalization. Show me you."

This you asking Bob to show you "Bob" and Bob's feverish pointing/insisting that he (pointing to himself) *is* Bob will go on for some time until Bob becomes a bit, or a lot, annoyed. The Deeply Philosophical Term for Bob's attitude at that time will be, "pissed off."

At this point, he will usually begin to assert—often forcefully and usually loudly—that this (pointing at himself) is "Bob," that "he" is "Bob," and that he ("Bob") is here, and sheeesh, what are you, dense, or *what?*

Next, he may begin to insist that his body is Bob. That his nose is Bob, or his hair, or his fingers, or his blood, or his brain—he may insist that one or all of them is Bob.*

Finally, he may even declare that his "soul" is Bob.

But you know that Bob ... isn't there.

A Pity to Say So

A student asked his Zen master if it was not so that the mountains were Buddha, the sky was Buddha, the trees were Buddha, and the very dew on the flowers was Buddha.

The master replied: "Yes. But it's a pity to say so."

*If you are *really* brave, you might remind him that every seven years, every cell in the human body regenerates itself, meaning that 100% of today's "Bob" is not the same "Bob" of seven-years-and-change ago. But, if you remind him of this, run!

Zen Do

Bob is a reason to meditate.

And as you meditate on Bob, take Bob apart: spleen here, toes there, brain in another pile over there. All done? Has Bob been taken apart completely? Good.

Now, remember that each of those items in each of those "piles of Bob" regenerated itself in the last seven years.

Next, recall how "you are what you eat"—a morsel of tuna today becomes protein tomorrow, which is expressed as, say, a cell in Bob's thyroid gland. From tuna to thyroid gland cell, it's all one continuous process of life—and of Bob.

Next, follow that chain of being from a fish that the tuna ate through the growth of the tuna, thru to the growth of Bob. Add in the chain of the sun driving the growth of plankton, which are eaten by the fish, which the tuna eats, which Bob eats.

Now, look at the "piles of Bob." Mentally, reconstruct "Bob" into his "human form." See how abstract, how arbitrary, how unnatural are the labels of the items in both the "piles of Bob" and "Bob" himself.

Not to mention the vocalization of the name, Bob.*

The point of all this chain-of-life chatter (aside from, you know, showing the chain-of-life..) is to illustrate how you,

*By the way ... you did keep notes on how to put ol' Bob back together again, right? I sure hope so, or he's really going to be pissed!

Bob, everything-there-is is not only related to one other, but is also a function of the universe that extends, uninterrupted and without pause, as far back into time as you wish to look (Big Bang, anyone?) and/or as far forward as the mind will allow.

You are all of eternity, from its most primordial sense to here-and-now-in-your-present-form expressed as (Insert Your Name Here.)

When you think about that, it's pretty damn amazing.

Not sure about that?

Ask Bob...

Singing Zen Harmony with the Temptations

From "Just My Imagination" by the Temptations:

Just my imagination, once again.
Running away with me.
Oh, I tell you, it was just my imagination,
Running away with me.

One of the issues people new to Zen grapple with centers in the terms "real" and "abstract" or "conceptual." Looked at from a certain perspective, the confusion is quite manifest.

So let's build that perspective here and see how we might help distinguish reality from imagination.

Our subject, Bob, is a hardworking plumber in Noblesville, Indiana, USA. He is thirty-nine years old and has a wife, two kids, and the requisite family dog. His family attends church when time allows*.

Our plumber works hard for his money and is thought of as a good, reliable worker who hunts, fishes, enjoys NASCAR, and belongs to the American Legion and VFW. He is, in all respects, what the media

*This Bob does *not* bite his nails.

and press refer to as a solid, upper-middle-class, blue-collar success and a solid citizen.

And he's deeply, although very privately and personally, unsettled and unhappy with his life.

He has a vague feeling of "Is That All There Is?" to life, to borrow another popular music lyric. He hasn't really shared this with his wife, whom he is, *he thinks*, still in love with. Because while he may be the right man to tackle heavy-duty plumbing, or hunt a half-ton moose, or put a weapon to his shoulder and defend his country in combat on foreign soil—he's, well, uncertain. He's not had all the practice he could have on how to express what he feels as opposed to what he thinks. Or of expressing what he *sees* as distinct from what he's been told to see.

Two Watts

Alan Watts famously quipped that the equator was a useful enough concept but it could never be used to tie up a package.

He said the same thing about the lines of longitude and latitude.

Zen Do

Much of what passes for "everyday life" is imaginary. To wit:

- No you don't need to believe in religion. Freedom of religion also means freedom from religion.
- No you don't have to go to school and get a four-year degree immediately after high-school. It's a handy thing to have, but I know lots of folks with Bachelors and Masters degrees who are, as my father used to say, "educated idiots." Whatever you want to do for a living—get the education you need to attain that.

- No you don't have to get married and have 2.3 kids and a family dog.
- No you don't have to work at the same job for 30 years.
- No you don't need to live in a house/apartment you can't afford. If you want to live in a yurt or a Buick, rock on.
- No you don't need to go to the 'right places' and be seen with the 'right people.'
- Yes if you want to have sex with 6, 16, or 66 people in your life, practice safe sex and go to it.
- It ain't all about the money. He who dies with the most toys doesn't win, he's a dead fucker who left behind a bunch of stuff for his family to clean up.
- Like Paris? Move there. Tomorrow.

The point is: there is no plan, no model, no script, no program, no guide, no entry or cheat sheet to reality.

Look and study the people who tell you there is: they're either selling something* or they exercise some sort of power, influence, or control as a function of fronting for whatever it is they are fronting for. Or, they are people who have believed it when they were told that this-is-the-way-it-is. Don't pity, or belittle, or hold them in contempt. They are unrealized Zen.

So who do you know who is walking through life playing a role they feel they didn't ask to be cast in?

Who do you know who is *screaming* inside for some peace not based on someone else's dogma, someone else's belief system, someone else's rules of the game?

*Call for Scientology!

Who do you know who is also singing/living, without realizing it, "It's just my imagination, running away with me?"

You?

Smothered in the Colorful Robes of Belonging

I have many friends who are "belongers"—they belong to a variety of groups. In fact, it seems as though their lives are defined by the groups they are in. Almost as if they need the group, or at least the "wrapper" of membership in the group, to define who they themselves are.

Talk to some of these "belongers" about Zen, for example, and they'll quickly tell you how they "got Zen." They "found it" after they joined a Yoga class on Tuesday and Thursday nights.

Discuss the human condition, and they'll describe how they "found their social conscience" after joining Habitat for Humanity or the American Civil Liberties Union.

Or you might hear:

"I can't stand people wearing fur. That's why I belong to People for the Ethical Treatment of Animals."

"I found God after I joined the Catholic Church."

"Poverty? Don't talk to me about it—I belong to a group that volunteers at St. Patrick's one day a month and every Thanksgiving."

To these folks, in their world, belonging is validation, definition, attainment, and sacrifice.*

Do Clothes Make the Man?

There's the story of a Zen master who wore his simple monk's robes to a dinner to which he had been invited. People from far and wide came to see this famous Zen teacher. There was much speculation about how ornate and expensive his robes would be, considering his vast reputation.

Upon his arrival, the master went to the front door of the event and was promptly stopped. The person who opened the door saw this commonly dressed elderly man as just another beggar and brusquely told him to go to the back door and beg! This was no place or time for beggars! Didn't this beggar know that an important Zen master was expected soon?

The master then went into the woods, and over his simple dress he slipped into an elegant, flowing silk robe, rich with intricate patterns, gold thread, and lavish decoration. Thus attired, he returned to the front door of the event.

This time, he was admitted and with much ceremony and deference was taken to a seat of honor. Everyone commented on what a striking figure he cut and how well his elegant apparel suited him.

Arriving at his reserved seat, the master immediately removed his princely robes, announced that he was leaving the assembly, and concluded by saying, "It is clear. Your honors are intended for the robes."

*Even if the sacrifice is writing a check.

Zen Do

People wrap themselves in layers of belonging, mistaking it for reality. They have also mistaken membership in a group for understanding. They've confused dogma for truth, and mistaken attendance for contribution. Wrapped in layers of belonging, they are mistaking the bread wrapper for the load of bread.

There's certainly nothing wrong with belonging to organizations. Especially to groups that help people.

But the next time you're in a group—look to see what type of robes the other "members" are wearing. And look at your robes, too.

Are you defining "us" and "them" or "good" and "bad" based on the "robes" someone else is wearing? Are you choosing winners and losers based on the conceptual criteria of the group?

Does belonging to a group set some people apart, however discretely*.

The path of Zen isn't called the middle way for nothing. Discrimination and choosing create stress, loss, desire, pain, and alienation from reality.

In your belonging, and in your Zen practice, are you the monk? Or are you the robe?

*Hint: You can't have an us without a them!

Speaking In Tongues

Right now—wherever you are, tell me something about, say, global warming.

Thanks.

Now—think about this for a moment: whose voice am I really hearing when you speak? Yours? Or someone else's?

When young, we tend to take our parents' views as pretty serious stuff.

And before you can say bada-boom-bada-bing, their thoughts are your thoughts.

A Side-Tracked Smile

Billy, a Zen student, told Pam, a Zen teacher, "Brilliancy of Buddha illuminates the whole universe."

Before he had even finished, Pam interrupted, "You are reciting someone else's poem, are you not?"

"Yes," answered Billy.

Shielding her eyes from the bright spring sun, Pam said, "You are sidetracked."

Billy frowned.

Dana, another Zen student standing nearby overheard this exchange and suddenly smiled.

Dana *saw*.

Zen Do

Take an active meditation session (one in which your aim is to focus on a given topic and to meditate just on/about that topic or issue) and meditate on the topic of this chapter: the voices in your head.

Do you sometimes hear your dad's words coming out of your mouth? Do you sometimes see your mom's words written in your hand? Was that your sister's voice who spoke out from you about this or that matter the other night?

Pick a topic—abortion, Zen, cars, alcohol, sex, money, race relations, nature, crime, poverty ... pick any subject and create a short list of, say, three things you think about that topic. Then ask yourself the questions "Why?" and "Where?"

Why do you believe those things, and where did those thoughts originate? Try to locate and isolate the source.

And when you locate and isolate the source, ask yourself: "Is my opinion/belief my voice—or theirs? And if theirs, why?"

Once you've isolated the source/voice, it's that much easier to leverage the two best words of advice I've ever received in my Zen study: "Let go."

But—when you can hear your voice inside yourself and see that it is based on your firsthand experience.—you'll know you're listening to the voice of Zen.

Listen.

Monkey Mind in a Zen Reduction

If you've stayed in any major hotel lately, you know how hard it can be to find a plain cup of basic Lipton tea*. Or a simple pork chop with unadorned mashed potatoes and a Caesar salad.

Everything seems more complicated than it needs to be: lemon tea with *mint infusion*. Pork loin *in a balsamic vinegar and ginger reduction*. Or, my Australian favorite, a cheeseburger with (*shudder*) red beets on it. (The heck with Zen: there's just something **wrong** with that one!)

I don't know about beets on burgers, but I do know there is no Top 10 Checklist of Right Choices, and neither life nor enlightenment comes in a Teacher's Edition containing all the "right answers."

If there were such a "One Book," would it be a work that describes an ethical system to live by? Would it be a functional (note that word) self-help book? Or a spiritual reference, with all that name implies? Or would such a book be a religious tome of appropriate insight?

That's a lot to ask of any one book. It's like asking the *New York Times* Best Seller *Smokin* by Mr. Myron Mixon (one of my personal

* I'm a Lipton tea and a Tejava guy from way back. They're the best; good, refreshing tea. I know—shameless product placements. Sue me.

heroes), to be the one and only cookbook for everyone for every meal.

You see the problem. There has to be a way to get insight without having to read chapter-and-verse or BBQ a whole hog (there's a mixed metaphor if ever I saw one...)

Live Zen, Dead Words

Once, Mason, who had just become a Buddhist monk lay down to sleep for the first time in his new bed in the monastery. He shared a very large bedroom with over a dozen other monks.

When the lights were out and everyone was tucked in, one of the monks in the far corner of the room yelled out. "9!" A moment later, all the monks giggled.

A minute later, another monk next to Mason yelled out, "101!" A moment later all the monks laughed loudly. Then someone yelled, "48!" All of the monks roared with laughter.

Mason was quite perplexed by now, but he decided to yell out a number as a gesture to fit in with everyone else. He yelled out, "26!" A moment later, all the monks groaned with displeasure. After that, everyone went to sleep.

The next morning, as the monks washed before meditation practice, Mason asked one of the older monks, "Why do people laugh when someone calls out a number at night before we go to sleep?"

The older monk answered, "For years we've told the same jokes before going to sleep. Our Zen jokes tend to take a very long time before you get to the punch-line. So after a while, we just memorized the jokes and gave them each a number. So this way it is easier and faster for us to tell and get to the laughs!"

"Oh, I see!" said Mason, with a smile. "But why did everyone groan when I called out the number 26?"

Shaking his head, the older monk said, "That is just a really bad joke!"

Zen Do

The eminent scientist and Really Cool Dude Albert Einstein would have appreciated shorthand numbering for jokes. You may recall that Einstein is supposed to have said something like, "Everything should be made as simple as possible, but no simpler."

Exactly so.

There's nothing wrong with mint infused tea if that's your choice. My point isn't that we should limit choice, but rather we should live and think as simply as possible, but no simpler.

When "even more simple" becomes more work that "simple", we've checked out of reality and are not living mindfully. We are, in effect, gilding the simple lily.

A cheeseburger and a glass Lipton iced tea, please. And if you don't want beets on your cheeseburger, then you don't have to.*

Check please!

* Saying no to that will raise your personal stock in my eyes!

Steve Hagen and the Zen of My Cat

For those of you who read copious amounts of material on Buddhism, you've no doubt run across the name of one of the greatest communicators of Buddhism alive today, in my humble opinion: Steve Hagen.

Master Hagen is, among other things, the best-selling author of a number of works on Buddhism. He also has unique gifts as a natural-born storyteller. He's funny, insightful, grounded, and clearheaded. His teachings on Zen are similarly clear and easy to understand.

For me*, written or spoken, reading/hearing this man is like listening to Mozart: no translation necessary—the work (read: voice/communication/expression/Zen) stands on its own and requires no further description, narration, or interpretation.

That said, I think Steve has also been channeling Zen lessons through my cat, Joshua.

I'll explain. In his book *Buddhism Pure and Simple,* Hagen says, "If you point out the moon to a cat, he probably won't look at the sky; he'll come up and sniff your finger."

*Your Hagen mileage may vary.

Exactly so!

And with that, Master Hagen has taught Joshua—and you and me—a valuable Zen lesson.

The Difference Between

A Zen teacher asked his new, anxious student: "Are you listening or waiting to speak? Are you experiencing or predicting? Do you see or are you guessing?"

Zen Do

When I point at the moon, Joshua does just what Steve said: he sniffs my finger. He doesn't attach significance to the pointing. He isn't looking for a sermon in the sky. He has no interest in deep philosophical matters. He isn't angling to impress anyone with his "deep understanding of Buddhism," he's not making an existential or metaphysical "statement," and he's not trying to "show" me anything, least of all Zen.

He sees a finger. He sees something. He sees …

He sniffs the finger. He sniffs something. He sniffs …

Just so and no more.

What a great Zen lesson.

Now, if I could just figure out how Joshua met Steve Hagen …

Still Zen Runs Deep

We're always in a rush these days.

And few rushes are "rushier," if that's a word, than the rush to try and prove to somebody—anybody—that we *know* something.

Our ego typically gets involved in our learning and just won't keep still until we're flapping our gums about having learned whatever we've been working on.

Call it human, and the way of the world, if you like. As for me, I call it what it is: a funky speed bump on the path to Zen.

A Smile That Took Ten Years

A certain Zen master was never known to smile. That is—until the day he died.

Knowing that it was his time to pass on, the master called his students to him and said, "You have studied under me for more than ten years. Show me your real interpretation of Zen. Whoever expresses this most clearly shall be my successor and receive my robe and bowl."

The master watched the face of each student keenly. No one said a word.

Finally, one student scooted closer to his teacher. Reaching out, the student pushed his teacher's bowl forward a few inches.

The master's face took on an even more severe look. "Is *that* all you understand?" he thundered. The student reached out and moved the bowl back to its original position.

The master smiled.

"You rascal," he said. "Take my robe and bowl. They belong to you now."

Zen Do

Haven't you noticed that as you life has gotten busier with career issues, kids, maybe volunteer activities, and so on that it seems like months and even years just fly by?

Do you find yourself saying something like, "I can't believe it's (fill-in-the-date-or-month) already! Where did the (month/year) go?"

It's probably fair to say that those days/weeks/months/years that have flown-by have not been what one might call "measured." Nor did you probably spend much time just watching sunsets or a full moon. Or just being.

Remember "haste makes waste"? The discipline it takes to see now, to experience here, to see reality takes time and effort. Give them to yourself —mindfully.

Any teacher would appreciate a student who had mastered this lesson.

Swimming with Dolphins, Whispering Zen Numbers

In the play (and the movie) *Stand and Deliver,* one of the students, a guitar player in a rock band, is awakened from a desktop nap by his teacher.

In a daze, the student says, "I was dreaming—my band and I were swimming with dolphins, whispering imaginary numbers, looking for the fourth dimension ..."

That's quite a nap.

Without Zen awakening, we're all swimming in a dream of our own construction. But worse than that, we're missing all the fun!

A Zen Master and a Duck Walk Into a Bar

A Zen master visiting New York City goes up to a hot dog vendor on the street and says, "Make me one with everything."

The hot dog vendor fixes a hot dog and hands it to the Zen master, who pays with a $20 bill.

The vendor puts the bill in the cash box and closes it.

"Excuse me, but where's my change?" asks the Zen master.

The vendor responds, "Change must come from within."

Zen Do

Alan Watts once said Zen stories are like jokes, you don't "get them" gradually, you get them all at once, in a flash.

I believe that when we laugh we are truly in the moment. not when we think about why the joke was funny, but rather in that instant when Mind tells us the joke is funny.

The moment of laughter is Zen. And we need more of both.

To wit:

Drink tea and nourish life.

With the first sip ... joy.

With the second ... satisfaction.

With the third ... peace.

With the fourth ... a Danish!

A Zen master once said to me, "Do the opposite of whatever I tell you."

So I didn't.

Wherever you go, there you are.

Your luggage is another story.

Be here now.

Be someplace else later.

Is that so complicated?

To Find the Buddha, look within.

Deep inside you are ten thousand flowers.

Each flower blossoms ten thousand times.

Each blossom has ten thousand petals.

You might want to see a specialist.

To practice Zen and the art of Jewish motorcycle maintenance, do the following: get rid of the motorcycle.

What were you thinking?

Be patient and achieve all things.

Be impatient and achieve all things faster.

Teaching a Boy with No Patience

Funny thing about the title of this chapter—depending on how you read it, where you put emphasis or parse the words, you can create several meanings, such as that this chapter concerns or is about:

- Teaching a boy who has no patience.
- Teaching a boy when you have no patience.
- Using something called "No Patience" to teach a boy.
- Teaching: A Boy with No Patience

... and so on. Each version creates a slightly different mental picture, a subtly different view of the situation.

Each version is also a word game, in a sense.

But for those not awake, word games are essentially what pass for life.

Zen Master in Green

(This story may be *just a bit familiar* to some of you ...)

One day a master was instructing his latest pupil. The student didn't seem to be grasping what the master was trying to get across. Yet again the master explained the lesson, and the following conversation occurred:

Student: "All right, I'll give it a try."

Master: "No! Try not. Do—or do not. There is no try."

Zen Do

The master? Yoda. The student? Luke Skywalker. Both characters from the *Star Wars* movie saga.

Yet the lessons here are as valid and as valuable as if delivered personally by Gautama Buddha. Or Darth Vader.

In Zen, there is no try. To try is to invoke an idea. To try is to, well, *try*, rather than do. You're *doing something* else (trying) instead of *doing* what you're supposed to be doing. You're thinking about the trying, not the doing. In point of fact, you're thinking, *not* doing. And that, in doing, in life, and in Zen (which are all of a piece), is not the best way to become a Zen—or a Jedi—master.

Or even just an awake individual.

As for the doing itself ...

Yoda's calling you ...

The Give Away Zen for Free on Thursdays in Phoenix, AZ

One of the things you become accustomed to when writing or speaking about Zen is people asking the question: "What is it like to really experience Zen?"

And so one tries to answer the question, usually in terms of describing what Zen is not rather than what it is. Over the years, I've learned that this chip-away-from-the-outside approach, like carving a statue from the outside of a block of stone in, usually works, to some degree.

Note the "to some degree" part of that statement.

Actually, I can't *really* answer the question. I mean, how can I convey *my* experience of Zen. It's mine—it's my life, my experience, in my mind. And I don't know about *your* life script, but mine has lots of plot twists, new actors popping in and out like guest stars, a fascinating story line, lots of emotional highs and lows, great special effects (marriage, divorce, childbirth, etc.), and plenty of action—but I'm the only one who "sees" and experiences this particular script/movie. And for me, this isn't a movie—it's reality unfolding in panoramic color right before my eyes.

Yet that's not the case for everyone.

For some people, reality, as they see it, depends on what they're doing at any given point in time. For example, for these folks, when they walk out of a movie theater, they step out of the dark of the theater with thoughts of the movie in mind and then—bang—thoughts of the troubles, concerns, doubts, problems, worries, hopes and/or fears currently in their life flood back into their mind, and they think something along the lines of: "Oh. Yeah—that's right. The *real* world."

Real? Hardly. But I'm not going to come down on an experience at the local Metroplex as not being conducive to Zen, far from it—it is another way of answering that question about experiencing "real" Zen—with popcorn and extra butter added in.

Another way of answering the question is to suggest that the questioner take a trip down Phoenix, Arizona, way. Why Phoenix? Because those friendly folks down that way give away Zen for *free* on Thursdays.

I'll Have a Large Diet Coke, a Popcorn, and Zen, Please

One morning, a Zen master noticed one of his students reading a book while eating breakfast. Smiling, he approached the student and said, "When eating, just eat. When reading, just read." The student nodded, closed the book, and finished his breakfast.

At lunch that day, the student noticed the Zen master eating lunch and—reading the newspaper. Somewhat surprised, he approached the master and said, "Master, I thought you said that when eating, one should just eat, and when reading, one should just read. And yet here you are eating *and* reading."

"Yes," the master replied, "I did tell you that. But what I didn't tell you is that when you eat and read, just eat and read." At this, it was the student's turn to smile, as he suddenly saw a little deeper into Zen.

Zen Do

For those people looking to "experience real Zen," a movie—or a trip to an art gallery, or a sporting event, for example—may be one of the surest ways to do just that.

For example, at the movies, while "just" watching the movie, you are actually experiencing Zen in the form of the universe, the galaxy, the solar system, the drift of the continents, the rotation of the earth, the pull of the moon, gravity, the miracle of your body, the loss of the illusion of time ... *and* your popcorn, your Diet Coke, the seat you're sitting in, your shifting emotions during the film, and, of course, the movie.

Moreover, when you watch the movie and are really absorbed by it, you readily suspend your usual habit of passing judgment on "the real world," you generally have no awareness of your day-to-day "troubles," you may even forget a sickness or injury, and you're ready to take in anything the movie dishes out as valid (note I didn't say real)—there's just you and Zen, unchecking, going straight ahead, totally engaged in the moment—and the popcorn.

Like you, I also Zen at the movies, but I also Zen at art galleries—like the one in Phoenix where they occasionally have free Thursdays, which allow me to view the art on display gratis. Imagine that: free art *and* free Zen. Now, that's a double feature!

Want to experience Zen of this type for yourself? It's easy: *see* a double feature at the movies. Or, *listen* to the Beatle's

White Album. Or, *experience* paintings in an art museum.

Don't think *about* the art, movie, or music. Just *see/experience*—that's all, nothing added.

Life, and art, are alive and, like water, will not be held prisoner by the net of your thoughts, just as the experience in a single frame of a movie cannot be held prisoner, even by the 80-foot-tall frame of the movie screen.

So, if you're looking for some real Zen, don't ask me for my experience. Go to a concert, a gallery or a movie. Or go to Phoenix: heck they give away Zen for free on Thursdays down there.

30 Odd Foot of Zen Grunts*

One of the people who gave me the inspiration to write this book struck a note of irony in me when he asked, "How come most of the quotes I read about Zen are from elderly Chinese or Japanese Zen master-type guys? Who else 'speaks Zen'?"

A note of irony chimed in me because of the countless examples of "speaking Zen" I've noticed, in people from all walks of life and in a host of countries, over the years.

Every day, you may encounter something someone said or wrote, or that you said or wrote, and in so doing you experience a bit of awakening. Few of those "authors" are, I suspect, "Zen masters". Let's take a peek.

---

*As for the chapter title, I'd like to tell you it's based on some deeply meaningful Zen koan, or has special significance in the history of Buddhism, or is the result of some deep insight I've had into some arcane and obscure "secret" of Zen. Not a chance. The Australian actor Russell Crowe is a member of a band called 30 Odd Foot of Grunts, and I was looking for a way to work Mr. Crowe into this book in the vague hope that he might read the book and invite me to Australia to discuss same. (Russell! G'day, mate! Ready when you are!)

Baker's Dozen Zen

1. "A man should look for what is, and not for what he thinks should be." —*Albert Einstein*
2. "First master your instrument. Then forget all that bullshit and play!" —*Charlie Parker*
3. "Man is the only animal for whom his own existence is a problem which he has to solve." —*Erich Fromm*
4. "In the presence of eternity, the mountains are as transient as clouds."—*Robert Green Ingersoll*
5. "Words, like eyeglasses, blur everything they do not make clear."—*Joseph Joubert*
6. "The more we live by our intellect, the less we understand the meaning of life."—*Leo Tolstoy*
7. "The butterfly counts not months but moments, and has time enough."—*R. Tagore*
8. "Art is frozen Zen."—*R.H. Blyth*
9. "You lose it, if you talk about it."—*Ernest Hemingway*
10. "If you want to make an apple pie from scratch, you must first create the universe."—*Carl Sagan*
11. "If you take a flower in your hand, and really look at it, it's your world for the moment." —*Georgia O'Keeffe*
12. "I have lived with several Zen masters—all of them cats." —*Eckhart Tolle*
13. "I never saw a wild thing sorry for itself."—*D.H. Lawrence*

Zen Do

The lessons, the ability of these individuals to "speak Zen" is manifest, and I admire their eloquence as well as their dharma lessons. You know—when you get right down to it, from you, to me, to Russell Crowe, we all speak Zen.

Grunt once if you agree.

Whole Wheat Pancakes with a Side of Zen

I had a bit of satori this morning while making whole wheat pancakes. Timely, actually, because it demonstrates how Zen:

- Is reflected in all aspects of everyday life
- Does not require anything besides mindfulness
- Brings an awareness to many of us of things heretofore unconsidered: why we do things

If Zen can do all that while making whole wheat pancakes, it makes one wonder what it could accomplish with a six-course meal!

See, I'm learning to cook and have been having one heck of a good time doing so except for one minor issue: I'm a messy cook trapped in a neat-freak body. I just live for spreading a new batch of lasagna from one end of my kitchen to another (and since my kitchen was designed by a woman who wrote cookbooks for a living, well, you can imagine what a mess that is).

But I'm stumped, and often angered, by one of the kitchen's most pedestrian creations: pancakes. It seems that no matter how I try, I can botch one aspect or another of these delicious delights with one spatula tied behind my back.

Today's transgression: getting whole wheat flour all over the countertop. I tried not to, but managed to get that fine, tan powder all *over* my counter in the act of measuring it and pouring it in a bowl. How hard can that be?

For me, today, hard enough. But, had I not been "flour challenged," I might not have had my small encounter with satori.

See, it dawned on me that I get frustrated when cooking whole wheat pancakes because ... I never do it the same way twice.

I'm always dropping out of the moment and recalling the last time I was cooking pancakes, and how I did something that didn't quite work, and how that frustrated me, and then .... *whoops*, there it is: while thinking of the then and there, I did something in the here and now that didn't work out right, either.

How I could have expected the result to be anything other than "whoops," I don't know.

To begin with, I wasn't even present at the whoops moment—I was looking at the past and trying (futilely) to avoid feelings of guilt, anger, denial, self-criticism, and so on.

So how did I expect to make proper pancakes now if I was living in the past at the same time?

But we do this sort of thing all the time, don't we?

Don't Try: Do

Above the gate outside a temple in Kyoto, Japan, are the carved-in-wood words "The First Principle." For generations, people have admired the artistry with which the words were written/carved over two hundred years ago.

The student tasked with writing the words in ink on paper patiently wrote over eighty-four drafts of the text—none of which escaped the critical eye of a teacher who was not the least bit shy about expressing his dissatisfaction with the work as the author labored at his task.

However, when the teacher left the room for a few moments, the student thought, "Now is my chance to escape his keen eyes!" and he wrote the words "The First Principle" with a mind free from distraction.

And the teacher's comment upon his return?

"A masterpiece!"

Zen Do

After my rather messy pancake attempt this morning, I saw the clarity of my lesson and my delusion. I immediately cleared away all the trappings of pancake making, left the room for a few moments to still my mind, and then came back into the kitchen and assembled all the materials needed to make whole wheat pancakes.

I measured, mixed, and cooked quickly, assuredly, and then and there. Small spills and splatters added dimension to the cooking art. I noticed them, then pulled my mind back to pancakes.

I do believe it was the most delicious Zen I've ever eaten.

Pancakes, anyone?

Zen Doorways

A door is a door is a door, right? Well, perhaps.

In some cases a door functions as a barrier. Other times as a locked vault. Other times as a band-aid. Many times as security. Still other times as a gateway. And sometimes—as a tombstone.

We each have many doors with myriad functions in our day-to-day mind. Some without locks, many with, and we'll talk about that more in a moment.

Have you reflected on how doors often form the last barrier between you and some fundamental event in your life? A few examples: The doors to an operating room. The door to the Oval Office in the White House. The door to the aisle of a church where your wedding is being held. The doors of a funeral parlor—the one where your funeral is being held.

Have you pondered how it is that doors speak louder (sometimes *much* louder) than words in conveying the emotional relationship between you and someone on the other side of a door—even, or especially, if the door is closed?

Speaking of emotions, few things speak louder than the slamming of a door. (I will only grace note the volumes, spoken and heard, said and unsaid, when a door is knocked or kicked off its hinges.)

On another front, many of us learn our first real concepts of privacy by being able to turn a knob and close the door to our bedrooms. On a related angle, what tales of intrigue, exploration, or discovery could be told by, or through, the humble keyhole?

From "Zen and the Art of Motorcycle Maintenance"

"The truth knocks on the door and you say, "Go away, I'm looking for the truth," and so it goes away. Puzzling."

—*Robert M. Pirsig*

Zen Do

Look for and at the doors in your house—and in your mind.

Your childhood home ... your first office ... your last office ... the barracks ... the dorm ... the funeral home ... the drunk tank ... the vice principal's office ... the house of your grandmother ... your first manager's office door ... the bathroom door she locked.

Some of these doors are open, some acre closed. Many may be locked with nary a key in sight. Some doors are hidden away, papered over, painted shut and will take all your focus to locate and open.

Open the doors—even if you have to kick them down.

What do you *see*? What do you feel?

Zen shows us that the thoughts, constructs, emotions, and evasions you thought were attached/manifested to or by that door are, when confronted, just as illusory as the monsters that, as a child, you were convinced lurked, ready to pounce, just behind your closet door.

So—you're standing at another doorway now, knob in hand. Read the label on the door. You may think you need all your ingenuity to deal with what's inside.

Use mindfulness instead.

Gently open the door.

Screw it—tear it off its hinges if you have to.

A lesson revealed.

Zen and the Death of the Yeahbuts

A common theme of this book is how folks have a wide variety of mechanisms for dodging *reality*. As I see it, it's almost as if, for many people, their reason for getting out of bed in the morning is to find, create, or wrap themselves in layer upon layer of "reasons" (read: excuses, justifications, validations, and/or rationalizations) as to why they should not or cannot do otherwise and are thereby constrained by "the way things are" from, say, living in the moment or experiencing the unity and clarity of Zen.

A random selection of just some of the more popular of the abovementioned layers of abstraction might include these jewels:

"Yeah, but … (insert explanation or rationalization here)," or

"That's because … (insert)," or

"You just don't understand … (insert)," or

"Well, see, it's like this … (insert)," or

"The thing is … (insert)," or

"It isn't like that, … (insert)," or

"You don't get it, do you? … (insert)," or

"This is the way it is …" or

Well, you get my point—and probably recognize the pattern.

These escapes from *here and now* are what I refer to as the Yeahbuts—code phrases for "I'm going to avoid *here and now* and cloak myself in said abstractions so as to purposely confuse them with *reality.*"

For example:

Amy: "So—how is your divorce going?"

Mary: "Oh, well, Larry's still living at the house."

Amy: "After three months? *Why?*"

Mary: "He hasn't gotten all the furniture for his new place yet."

Amy: "Mary, he's using you."

Mary: Yeah, but I'm just trying to be nice. Besides, you don't understand ………" … and so on.

Somewhat simplistic, I grant, but again you get my point.

Every single Yeahbut (or one of its companions from the list above) drops you out of *reality* and into a privately rationalized world all your own. As we can tell from the example just cited, such a world is headed for a painful awakening of its own, with the same certainty of an oncologist giving a terminal lung cancer prognosis.

I know that example is a bit … vivid, but that's intentional.

It's hell trying to invoke a Yeahbut when you're dead. On the other hand, how can one claim to have been truly alive when one has slept through one's life simply for wont of having not wanted to awaken to *reality.*

And waking isn't something we should "yeah, but ..." about. I mean, imagine this person's last thought upon realizing that (s)he has essentially (or actually) slept his or her life away: panic, frustration, the sense of drowning under the weight of realization that what was once there (if hidden by the dreams of delusion) is now *SO CLEAR!*

(S)he screams for another try, rips at his or her previous belief structure, destroying it and choking on the bitter dust of realization that as (s)he sees it, it's too little, too late. See this person begging to be given a chance to do it all over again now—one can almost feel the suffocation of death and the desperate clawing, grasping, screaming, blind panic of his or her last thought: "Yeah, but now I get it! ...."

Again, vivid—I agree. And, *yeah*, chock-full of concepts, thinking, imagination, and all manner of things "not Zen"—*but*, as I see it, better the nightmare of third-rate horror prose* to get even a *little closer* to awakening.

Cutting Through to Reality While Carving Up an Ox

A cook named Tom was cutting up an ox for Mayor Sage.

With every touch of his hand, every heave of his shoulder, every move of his feet, every thrust of his knee—zip! zoop!—he slithered the knife along with a zing, and all was in perfect rhythm, as though he were performing a intricate dance or keeping time to complex jazz changes.

"Ah, this is marvelous!" said Mayor Sage. "Imagine skill reaching such heights!"

Cook Tom laid down his knife and replied, "Skill is a minor part, Mr. Mayor. What I care about is the Way, which goes beyond skill."

*I almost expected myself to write, "It was a dark and stormy night ..."

"When I first began cutting up oxen, all I could see was the physical ox itself. After three years, I no longer saw the whole ox."

"And now—now I go at it by spirit and don't look with my eyes. Perception and understanding have come to a stop and spirit moves where it wants. I go along with the natural makeup, guide the knife through the big openings, and follow things as they are. So I never touch the smallest ligament or tendon, much less a main joint."

"A good cook changes his knife once a year—because he cuts. A mediocre cook changes his knife once a month—because he hacks. I've had this knife of mine for nineteen years and I've cut up thousands of oxen with it, and yet the blade is as good as though it had just come from the grindstone. There are spaces between the joints, and the blade of the knife has really no thickness. If you insert what has no thickness into such spaces, then there's plenty of room—more than enough for the blade to play about it. That's why after nineteen years the blade of my knife is still as good as when it first came from the grindstone."

"However, whenever I come to a complicated place, I size up the difficulties, tell myself to watch out and be careful, keep my eyes on what I'm doing, work very slowly, and move the knife with the greatest subtlety, until — flop! the whole thing comes apart like a clod of earth crumbling to the ground. I stand there holding the knife and look all around me, completely satisfied and reluctant to move on, and then I wipe off the knife and put it away."

"Excellent!" said Mayor Sage. "I have listened well and have just learned not only how to focus, but how to live, and how to nurture life."

Zen Do

Look at your own life and ruthlessly root out the Yeahbuts.

Focus is an amazingly powerful tool, yet most of us barely learn to harness it in our lives. Focus is the spark of creativity. Focus is what makes us mindful and in the moment. Focus can be learned, strengthened, and even taught through mindfulness studies and through meditation.

But focus is fragile, and without training, it can vanish like a mirage before our eyes. We're still looking, but we cannot see. For many of us, this is when we substitute (and focus on) a Yeahbut. Or two. Or twenty...

Learning to focus your mind also allows you to focus on the good, the beauty, and the myriad things that make up our universe, thereby eliminating excuses and negativity and enhancing our lives. This is not some Pollyanna Principle at work, seeing/remembering only the pleasant things in life.

Rather, this is focusing on beauty (as you see it, Mr./Ms. Beholder) and really seeing it, studying it, knowing it, and embracing it. It is also saying, in effect, "Yeah, I know there is negativity and ugliness in my life as I see it, but I'm going to simply recognize it when I see it, let it pass, and return to the beauty around me."

As a man said, "If we could see the miracle of a single flower clearly our whole life would change." (Gautama Buddha.)

And yes—I did just turn a negative principle (the Yeahbut) into a positive experience. That wasn't a rationalization on the part of Your Friendly Neighborhood Author, that was seeing reality and using a specific tool to help me/us see it with added purpose.

We'll never carve an ox if we hide behind the rationalizations of Yeahbuts.

Zen/reality: no ifs, ands, or buts of any kind.

Zen and the Eye of the Beholder

There is a natural tendency for people new to Zen to come to the practice more or less in sync with the following train of thought about what constitutes "real Zen teaching" and "real Zen teachers."

"Real Zen teachers" and "real Zen instruction" …

- "…must come from someone who has studied Zen at the knee of yet another learned master—preferably for decades."
- "…has to come from someone of Asian, preferably Japanese, Chinese, or perhaps Tibetan, descent."
- "…must be delivered by someone who looks the way a Zen master is supposed to look." Typically, and with full credit to their craft, this means a Zen master should look like, say, David Carradine from the '70s TV series *Kung Fu*. Or one of his masters in that TV show, elegantly clad in black or orange robes and fairly dripping with Extreme Gravitas.
- "…must be measured by the ability of the student to deliver complete lectures and recitations of "real Zen" as concisely as possible

based on the Zen instructor's own dissertations on the subject."

- "...must only be based on the *pick-your-brand-of-Buddhism's-favorite-books-here* texts."
- "...must be received by someone who has been ordained a Zen monk. Then a Zen priest. Then a Zen master."
- "...must not deviate in any way from the documented teachings of the ancients."
- "...must not deviate in any way from the teaching of *insert-your-favorite-Zen-writer-or-teacher-here.*"
- "...must be in lockstep with the words and writings attributed to the Buddha."

Yet ... real Zen couldn't be further from that list if it tried.

An Excellent Lesson

A young physician happened to meet a friend who had been studying Zen. Curious, the young doctor asked his friend what Zen was.

"I can't tell you that," the friend replied, "but I can tell you one thing: if you understand Zen, you will not be afraid to die."

"That is an excellent lesson," the doctor said. "Where can I find a teacher?"

His friend suggested his own Zen master. The doctor went to see the master straightaway, carrying a large and very sharp dagger so as to see for himself if this Zen teacher was afraid to die.

When the Zen master saw the doctor, he said, "Well, hello, friend. How are you? We haven't seen each other for a long time!"

The doctor was confused. "But we have never met before."

"That's right," said the Zen master. "My mistake. I took you for another physician who is also receiving instruction here."

Feeling somewhat at a loss, the doctor decided not to try and test the master, so he rather reluctantly asked if he might receive Zen instruction.

The Zen master said, "Of course. Zen is not difficult. Here is your lesson: if you are a physician, treat your patients with kindness. That is Zen." With that, the Zen master rose and left the room.

The doctor visited the Zen master three more times, and each time the master told him the same thing: "A physician should not waste time around here. Go home and take care of your patients. Treat them with kindness."

By his fourth visit, the doctor complained, "My friend told me that when one learns Zen, one loses the fear of death. Each time I come here, all you tell me is to take care of my patients. I know that much. If that is your so-called Zen, I am not going to visit you anymore."

The Zen master smiled, nodded, and said, "I have been too strict with you. Let me give you a koan," and he presented the doctor with a koan to work over.

The doctor pondered this koan for two years. At length, he thought he had reached certainty of mind. But his teacher commented, "You are not in yet."

The doctor continued in his concentration for another year and a half. During this time, his mind became placid, problems dissolved, No-Thing became the truth, he served his patients well, treated his patients (and everyone else he came in contact with) with kindness, and, without even knowing it, became free from concern over life and death.

At length, he went to visit his Zen master once again.

Taking one look at him, the old teacher just smiled.

Zen Do

In Zen, your role is as the doctor in our story. Showing compassion without discrimination. Helping all beings in whatever we do, and/or whenever we can.

There are no entrance exams for being a Zen teacher and no thesis to write or dissertation to be droned on about. Strip away all the clutter and clatter about how one is "supposed" to learn "real Zen" and whom one is supposed to learn it from, and you'll soon realize that Zen is found the same way beauty is: in the eye of the beholder.

Look: Zen.

Zen Enlightenment in F-Sharp Minor

People often fall into the habit of thinking that quantity or volume (of words, music, reading, speaking, or study, for example) means insight.

By extension, folks often feel that to properly and completely convey a subject to an audience, a teacher or expert must deliver a detailed product of his or her expertise—a lecture, a series of scholarly tomes, a suite of symphonies, or the like.

As a computer programmer, I coined the saying, "For many users, the value of a computer-generated report is directly proportional to the total weight of the the printed output of the report." Give many an executive the choice between a computer-generated report on a single piece of paper and a report of 843 pages, and he or she will tend to believe that the larger report must have more "value" because of its size—even if both reports convey the same conclusions.

In short, for many people, volume equals value.

Yeah—not so much.

Dharma in a Single Note

A Zen master, who was the first Japanese to study Zen in China, returned to Japan after many years of study. Once back in Japan, the emperor heard about the master and asked to be instructed in Zen by him.

So it was that the master arrived and stood before the emperor, saying nothing. Finally, he reached into the folds of his robe and produced a flute. He then blew one short note.

Bowing politely, he left.

Zen Do

Less is more.

What key is your life in?

(And the sound of a flute playing a single delicate note..........)

The Zen of Claude Rains

The other night, I was watching a movie called *The Invisible Man* starring the actor Claude Rains (most people remember him best in the role of Prefect of Police in another movie, *Casablanca,* with Humphrey Bogart). Watching the movie, I, like countless folks before me, let my mind wander into wondering what it would be like to be invisible.

To begin with, I thought it would sure make it tough to get a table at a restaurant. And even if I did grab a seat, it'd sure be *darn* hard to get the waiter's attention for more BV Rutherford Cabernet Sauvignon*.

That's when my mind, Claude Rains, the wondering, the wandering, and a quote by Richard Baker all came together and led me toward writing this chapter for you... the real Invisible Man.

Mr. Baker wrote, "Zen mind is one of those enigmatic phrases used by Zen teachers to make you *notice* yourself, to go *beyond the words* and wonder what your own mind and being are."

* Yep, another obvious product placement. I'm so ashamed...

Zen and the Way of Being Time

Katagiri Roshi wrote a book entitled "Each Moment is the Universe: Zen and the Way of Being Time."

Each moment is the universe—is a transcendentally viable—and visible—lesson.

Zen Do

That's who you are. You are the universe—at a place called here and now. Think about that. You are the universe—at a place called here and now. Most of us think of our lives as small. Perhaps even insignificant. We often think of ourselves as invisible in The Grand Scheme of Things. Ha! Far from it!

Re-read this chapter. Twice. You'll never be invisible again.

Where's that waiter with my Cabernet?

The Zen of Mozart's Breath

Water. H_2O. The essence of 70-odd percent of your being. If anything might, it alone can lay an almost indisputable claim to the phrase "the elixir of life." That much you've probably considered.

But, have you ever considered the Zen of water? I have—and the result was a watershed of insight.*

You see, scientists tell us that once created, nature never destroys water.

Today's rain, yesterday's condensation on the leaves of trees. Today's condensation, yesterday it was the moisture that evaporated from Mozart's breath as he labored over *The Magic Flute*.

Today's swimming pool contents, yesterday's ice age ice melted. Tonight's ice in your glass of twelve-year-old Scotch, yesterday's steam from Nero's burning of Rome.

Yep—the water you drink today, the water that resides inside, say, the tissue of your brain, may be the same (H) hydrogen and (O) oxygen that flowed in the Sea of Galilee in the days of Jesus Christ. Or it

*Sorry, I couldn't resist.

may be water contained in a snowflake that fell on George Washington as he crossed the Potomac.

Most of us never even think about water except in the sense of how we use it or how it operates (rivers, lakes, rain, monsoons, etc.). We're that abstracted from reality.

Moreover, most of us feel, to one degree or another, a sense of concepts like *then, ancient history, old, new, birth, death, rebirth, creation, destruction, enough,* and *waste.*

These, too, abstract us from reality because they try to fix reality in a concept, to "place" the world—or water—in a given place/time/setting/position. And in Zen we learn the absolute futility of attempting to catch the world in a net of abstractions and concepts because reality simply *is.*

So is water.

A Drop of Zen

A Zen master asked a student to bring him a pail of water for his bath.

The student did so, then poured the leftover water onto the ground.

"You dunce!" the master scolded him. "Why didn't you give the rest of the water to the plants? What right have you to waste even a drop of water?"

With that, the student gained enlightenment—and went on to change his name to a word that means "a drop of water."

Zen Do

How many times have you touched, consumed, seen, or felt water today?

Did you waste it?

Or use it?

Enjoy it?

Curse it?

Or did you see it as it is—always and forever standing right out in the open, pointing directly and unerringly to/at enlightenment?

All water has value as all life has value—and none should be wasted. After all, that's the kind of respect one should have, when dealing with Mozart's breath.

Author's Note: OK, OK, I give. Scientists tell us that, strictly speaking the hydrogen and oxygen in water are broken apart and reformed in to more (other?) water all the time, and that this has always been the case since Day One. My point is ... mine is a good story, so ease-off with the Mr. Science Guy stuff, will ya'?

Zen Sands Through the Hourglass

I've always had a fascination with clocks and time.

For me, the appeal of clocks is not in the considerable workmanship, or their elegance or decorative beauty, nor does my fascination for time result from the more pedestrian utility of, you know, telling time.

Nope. Clocks, and by extension time, as we use the term in daily life, fascinate me because they illustrate the true spirit of Zen with staggeringly beauty, elegant simplicity, and flawless argument.

I'll explain. (If you'd like a little musical accompaniment while you read, may I suggest "Does Anybody Really Know What Time It Is?" by Chicago, from their album *Chicago Transit Authority*.)

For many folks, a "year" is divided into twelve "months." Said months are further divided into a number of "weeks." Those weeks are made up of "days," a "day" is made up of twenty-four "hours," an hour of sixty "minutes," and a minute of sixty "seconds."*

*OK, so I'm a master of the blindingly obvious. Let's move on.

However, in Ethiopia, a year consists of twelve months—of thirty days each. The Ethiopians also add a five-day period (and even six days in leap years) called "Pagume." I don't know about you, but there's not one of those on my calendar.

OK, let's try the Hebrew world. Hang on—the Hebrew calendar is a couple of centuries older than the one you and I use. Next.

OK, forget calendars, surely we can all agree on time?

Whoops. Back in the ancient days of the Hebrew world, days begin at 6:00 PM, not 12:00 AM. Even hours are divided into 1,080 "helaqim," each of which is equal to 3½ seconds in length.

On the planet Jupiter, a day is ten earth hours long, not 24, and a year is twelve Earth years long. On the moon, a day and a year are the same thing. (A dayear? A yearday?)

OK—what about weeks? Certainly we can agree on those, right?

Well ... not so fast. According to countless calendars on countless walls, weeks all start on Sunday. Yet according to the International Standards Organization (ISO), weeks all start on Monday.

So you see the problem. Does anyone really know what time it is?

Zen on a 3-2 Count

Sometimes a Zen story has a more modern origin. In this story, baseball great and pitcher Tom Seaver is the student, and his coach Mr. Berra is the master.

Tom Seaver: "Hey, Yogi, what time is it?"

Yogi Berra: "What? You mean now?"

Zen Do

Zen brings you back to all the time you need: now. That's all the 'time' there ever has been.

Besides—I know I'm right on this one. I have Zen master Yogi's word on it.

Zen to the Left, Zen to the Right

When you turned the page to get to this chapter, did you use your left hand or your right?

When you kissed you child good-night last night, did you kiss him or her on the left cheek or the right?

When you washed your hands the last time you went to the bathroom, did you use the soap on your right or left hand first?

Based on the puzzled looks I'm sure this page, and those questions, are getting right now, I think I should just cut to the Zen story ...

An Umbrella Full of Zen

A Zen monk went to visit his master one rainy day. The monk was preparing to go out into the world to teach and wanted to take leave of his master.

His master greeted him with a question: "Did you leave your wooden clogs and umbrella on the porch?"

"Yes," said the monk.

"Tell me, then," the master said, "did you place your umbrella to the left of your shoes or to the right?"

The monk had no answer.

And, he knew he wasn't going out into the world quite yet. Clearly, his studies with his teacher were not complete and, most importantly, neither was his mindfulness practice.

Zen Do

Just like the Zen monk, the issue at hand (pun intended) is mindfulness.

And just like the Zen monk, you might also have thought you were completely present, completely mindful, and completely aware of something as simple as, say, which hand yyou used to turn a page in this book. But, perhaps not.

That being said, please allow me to derail one train of thought right here: the issue is mindfulness and not being able to remember and/or recite a litany of a thousand "How I Did It" laundry lists.

Zen—is as simple as turning a page, *mindfully*.

Acknowledgments

Zowie; this book has been a long time coming. And several people need to be recognized for their invaluable assistance in making it happen. To wit:

Sarah Clarehart: Thanks for the great book design, common sense advice, and laughs.

Brian Boles: Thanks, Bro, for kicking my ass when I needed to be working on this book. Silos needed!

W.E.B. Griffin: Thanking you, sir, for inscribing "Finish the damn book!" on one of your book jackets at a book signing in Scottsdale, Arizona after we had discussed how long I'd been at work on the manuscript for this book.

Alan Watts: For setting my dharma wheel spinning, thanks always.

Steve Hagen: Thanks, Steve, for showing me how writing about Buddhism should be done.

Barbara: Thanks, Mom. Without you…

Laura: Thanks, for always being there and for always believing.

Parker: Uber Tracker, you're my inspiration. Love, Dad.

—Kris Neely

Printed in Great Britain
by Amazon